chris lewyn

TENNIS

for
s real

the common sense training manual

A & C BLACK • LONDON

To MS
whose influence has touched far more
people than she has even met.
CS

First published 2005 by
A & C Black Publishers Ltd
37 Soho Square, London W1D 3QZ
www.acblack.com

ISBN 0 7136 7210 2

A CIP catalogue record for this book is available from the British Library.

Typeset in 9.5pt DIN-regular

Note: Whilst every effort has been made to ensure that the content of this
book is technically accurate and as sound as possible, neither the author
nor the publishers can accept responsibility for any injury or loss sustained
as a result of use of this material.

Text and cover design by Jocelyn Lucas
Cover image © 2005 JupiterImages Corporation
Photographs on pages vi, 27–35, 38–74, 81(bottom)–85, 90–94, 104, 112–17
© Mike King
Photographs on pages 37, 77–81 (top), 98–103, 107–9 © Grant Pritchard.
Photographs on pages 10, 23, 24, 50, 166 and 168 courtesy of Prince.

A & C Black uses paper produced with elemental chlorine-free pulp,
harvested from managed sustainable forests.

Printed and bound by GraphyCems in Spain.

Acknowledgements

The team would like to acknowledge the kind help and assistance of the following people, without whom this objective would have been unachievable:

Once again to Hannah and all at A&C Black for their continuing support.

Prince Tennis for their support with the photo shoot.
(Local stockists can be found at www.princetennis.com).

Eleiko and Specialist Sports for their kind donation of kit for the weightlifting shoot. (Specialist Sports can be contacted on +44 (0) 1590 681810).

And the models:

Greg Dunson – RAF 400 m and 110 m hurdles Champion and the winner of more RAF individual titles than any other athlete on record.

Mick Cartwright – five times 85 kg World Record holder and World Masters Weightlifting Champion (1999 & 2000).

Sue Lloyd – six times and Current English 58 kg weightlifting Champion. West Midlands and Great Britain squad member.

Anthony Rudd – Nottinghamshire County Champ, 400m hurdles.

Anna Sheryn – weightlifting and Pilates instructor.

Nick Morgan – resident tennis specialist and current holder of the LHP Trophy.

CONTENTS

About Lilleshall

The Lilleshall Sports Injury and Human Performance Centre is based at the Lilleshall National Sports Centre in the heart of the Shropshire countryside. It provides training and competition facilities to a wide range of sports, and provides specialist sports injury rehabilitation for injured professional athletes of all sports.

Lilleshall staff are involved in wide-ranging educational and media work, and the centre is committed to delivering practical sports science and sports medicine support to both coaches and athletes. The interaction between the centre's physiotherapists and sports scientists in achieving this objective is unique in the UK.

Lilleshall currently offers the only residential sports rehabilitation centre in the UK. Clients are referred to us from all areas of elite sport. Our science support services include fitness and physiological testing, nutritional advice and training prescription.

The centre operates across sports categories and with organisations such as:

- the Lawn Tennis Association
- the National Squash Racquets Association
- the English Table Tennis Association
- the Professional Footballers Association
- the British Gymnastics Association
- the British Paralympics Association
- the Motor Sports Association
- the Jockey Club
- the UK Premier and Football Leagues
- many UK Premier and Football League soccer clubs
- amateur and professional rugby players of both codes.

The centre can be contacted about courses and treatment via its website (info@lilleshall.com).

About the team

Chris Sheryn A highly experienced consultant from the field of international commerce, Chris designs and runs coaching programmes and specialises in the development of juniors. His work with Lilleshall and Conrad Phillips (see below) over recent years has helped to emphasise the need for an authoritative but concise resource for the thousands of players who have to balance life and sport but still want to improve their game.

Sam Howells Sam is a graduate of Loughborough University and holds a BSc in Physical Education and a Master's degree in Sports Science. Her duties as Senior Sports Physiologist at the centre involve support for wheelchair athletes and organisations as diverse as those involved with British gymnastics to the Castrol/Honda motor sports teams. A well-published writer on many areas of sports science, Sam has a high level of experience supporting many elite athletes in a wide variety of sporting arenas.

Conrad Phillips Former Great Britain and RAF team coach, Conrad is a UK athletics coach and a BWLA instructor. He has produced a national medal winner, an international athlete or a British record holder every year since he began coaching in 1969. He is chairman of the Staff Coach Council and tutor for the new UKA Coach Education. Conrad is a former 100 m champion.

Phil Newton Phil is director of the centre and a Chartered and State Registered Physiotherapist. Specialising in sports injuries and rehabilitation he has been working with elite athletes from many sports for over 15 years. He is head of the Professional Footballers Association Rehabilitation Centre and a member of the Lawn Tennis Association Physiotherapy Committee. Phil is also the England squash team physiotherapist.

Pauline Newton A Chartered and State Registered Physiotherapist, Pauline has a wealth of experience working in injury rehabilitation; indeed, there are few in the UK that have more experience helping athletes return to competitive action. Pauline's most recent experience has seen her work with international racquet sports squads from around the world.

Foreword

Over recent years tennis at the highest level has undergone a number of dramatic changes. One of the most marked is the rise to prominence of the 'tennis athlete'. These are players that treat 'dry-side' or off-court conditioning and preparation with the same meticulous attention as that of a track and field athlete. Not surprisingly, such players find an edge in their ability to maintain high levels of performance even in the most demanding of environments.

Of course many professionals have the luxury of time and opportunity – banks of sports scientists, physiotherapists and specialist coaches attend to every element of their off court preparation. This is not something that is readily available to all levels of club players across the country. However, just as Formula One race cars contribute to the development of family saloons there are elements of elite conditioning that can be adapted to become relevant and applicable to players of all standards and ages.

Therefore the million dollar question for most players, be they social or competitive, is 'what can I do first to make the maximum difference to my game?' For the thousands of club players there is always likely to be tension between sport, home and work. I was therefore delighted when the guys at Lilleshall Human Performance Centre revealed that they have been working on the adaptation of conditioning programmes to meet the needs of the tennis community as a whole.

There is, without doubt, relevance in these pages for all players who want to get that little bit more out of their game. Whilst high level performers can benefit from the concepts and drills, what is really innovative here is that now the information is not limited to the elite group but can be used by all – be they young or old, aspiring contenders or social players.

David Felgate

Who is this book for?

This book is *not* a technical tennis manual.

This book will *not* tell you how to deliver the perfect forehand and does not pretend to offer guidance on how to make that tricky overhead. What this book *can* do, however, is to offer you the off-court physical preparation advice that will help you succeed. The conditioning programmes here are designed to build a platform from which you can deliver your tennis skills more effectively.

This book *does* take account of the fact that 99.9 per cent of players have to balance work, family and social life with their tennis. It is aimed at the person who enjoys tennis as a single part of a varied life. What is provided here is a concise reference for those who want information that they can understand easily and quickly, so that they can then use it to help in their quest to ensure that they get all that they want out of their game.

Traditionally, off-court conditioning has been the preserve of the elite player. And indeed many players see tennis as a way of 'getting fit' rather than a sport for which they need to prepare. There are no presumptions in this book as to which position is of greater value, and what defines success will be different for every player. Equally, what role conditioning will play will vary from person to person. The principle at the heart of this book is that whatever your objectives, whatever your circumstances and whatever your available time and facilities, you can train for tennis. Here are just a few sample situations:

I am 48 and always dread the stiffness that accompanies the days following the first game of the season. I just want to train for an hour or two a week during the winter to ensure that I enjoy my season. Unfortunately, I work away from home a great deal and can't always get to an indoor court or a gym.

I have a young family and I play twice a week. That doesn't leave me enough time to do any off-court training, although I feel my enjoyment of the sport would increase if I could do something to prepare.

My teenage son/daughter is mad keen and I would like to know what conditioning work will be beneficial and safe for them. They already spend significant time on court playing and with our coach, but an hour two or three times a week at home would be really useful.

I am currently playing at county level and am looking for a physical edge. I am prepared to commit a significant amount of time each week to off-court work.

At the Lilleshall Centre we have been working with professional and elite amateur athletes for many years and it is this experience that is behind the structure of the book you are about to read. It is very important that each area is treated with equal importance and that you do not skip to the bits that you think are important. Think of this book as a map: like any map it describes a path as well as a destination, and in the world of sports-specific conditioning *there are no shortcuts*. Those who try to find them are the people that keep our injury clinic fully booked!

Special considerations

The assumption that all players are the same would be as wrong as to assume that everyone's objectives are the same. Every player is starting from a different point of fitness, flexibility, strength, and so on. Finding your own current position and areas of strength and weakness will be dealt with in the next chapter.

Before we get to that there are four key groups of players who are worthy of special mention here, and for whom special considerations should be made when reading and using this book.

1. pre-adolescents

2. adolescents

3. women

4. seniors.

As the book progresses I will describe the suitability of the activities under discussion for each of these groups.

The first two groups involve children, who can be subdivided into pre-adolescents and adolescents.

Pre-adolescents

The most important aspect of training the young people in this group should be *variety*.

From the age of eight to thirteen (referred to in athletics as 'the Golden Age of Skill Learning') children should try every possible sport and every possible physical activity they can – as long as it's legal and safe to do so!

Children should not be pressured by over-eager parents or coaches to be excessively competitive – more children drop out of tennis because of too much parental pressure to do better than their maturation allows than ever stay in the sport. Just as a large vocabulary will enhance educational advancement, the bigger the movement vocabulary, the greater will be the ability to acquire new skills and to excel in whatever sport is eventually chosen.

Generally speaking, pre-adolescent children are flexible and weak (in relative terms). It is therefore not necessary to get them to do any formal flexibility work. They are also, by nature, aerobic animals and have no anaerobic capacity, so neither is it appropriate for them to do any formal strengthening work. However, their tennis 'technical' work should emphasise appropriate movement patterns, which in themselves will have a 'strengthening' effect (for example, throwing activities to strengthen and to teach appropriate patterns of movement).

It is also an age where habits are learned and thus it is a good idea to introduce some of the movements that may, in later life, be used at greater intensity.

Adolescents

The first point to make is that in this group the chronological age of an individual may be up to five years out of sequence with an age-matched counterpart. It is therefore imperative that any physical conditioning/sport training be individualised. That is to say that those organising group training sessions should not assume that all players are of equal ability or capacity.

Adolescents are generally the opposite to their younger counterparts with respect to their overall physical profile (that is, they are relatively strong and inflexible). These characteristics will be more pronounced throughout growth spurts. Flexibility work is generally a good idea and specific attention (especially during and just after growth spurts, when muscle length can lag behind increases in long bone length) should be paid to the hamstrings and calf muscles as tightness in these muscle groups has been linked to episodes of anterior knee pain – very common in adolescents, especially girls.

Strength training has always been a contentious subject with this age group. Many books and coaches believe that such activities render players inflexible and can even stunt the growth of young players. There is no evidence for such generalisations. However, if children attempt adult schedules they will develop compensatory (almost always bad) habits. On the other hand, if it is taught well and *progressed* sensibly, strength training (in relation to body weight/free exercise) is a positively beneficial activity.

Even if tennis is chosen early as the first sport, then circuit training, jogging, skipping, medicine ball, appropriate jumping and agility exercises, and weight lifting and training that emphasise the technical excellence of each exercise rather than intensity of it should be undertaken – as should football, swimming, basketball, martial arts, cycling and as many other sports as feasible; the end result will be a fit, well-developed all-round young athlete with:

- increased resistance to injury
- reduced likelihood of hitting discouraging plateaux
- the potential to achieve their potential!

Competition before the child is physically or emotionally ready will always have a seriously detrimental effect on that child's ultimate success.

Women
PLAYING/TRAINING AND THE MENSTRUAL CYCLE

Through personal experience you will no doubt have an understanding of how much your menstrual cycle can affect your performance. While you cannot alter your cycle to fit in with training and playing, it is important to understand what is going on with your body and why. Here comes the 'science bit', so brace yourself... There are three phases to the menstrual cycle:

1. follicular (from day 1 to 13)

2. ovulation (day 14)

3. luteal (from day 14 to 28).

Each phase has differing hormone levels associated with it. Oestrogen is believed to affect performance and its concentration is low during the follicular phase, peaks at ovulation and is higher and more stable during the luteal phase.

Oestrogen affects the type of fuel most readily available for the working muscles. The way that the muscles are fuelled can affect training and performance. Low levels of oestrogen favour the breakdown of carbohydrate, whereas high levels favour fat breakdown.

Therefore in the follicular phase, where carbohydrate is favoured, tempo work, speed runs and interval training will feel easier, whereas in the luteal phase, where fat is favoured, longer, slower runs will feel easier. So don't beat yourself up if your performances vary throughout the month – look on your progress month on month rather than week to week as the playing field does not remain even throughout your cycle.

MENSTRUAL DYSFUNCTION

It is estimated that up to 44 per cent of athletic females may experience some changes in their cycle or even experience the cessation of their periods at some point in their career. This brings with it fertility problems, an increased risk of stress fractures and an increased risk of osteoporosis. Very often, menstrual irregularities are linked to weight loss, low caloric intake and increased physical training. However, you do not have to be an elite athlete to suffer from these problems: many runners who only consider themselves to be 'average' may be affected as there is a very fine line between a healthy level of exercise and too much. One worrying finding of some research is that many runners believe that menstrual dysfunction is a normal part of physical training – *this is not the case.*

INJURY RISK

As mentioned above, female players are far more prone to injuries of one of the key stabilising ligaments of the knee – the anterior cruciate ligament (ACL) – than are their male counterparts. In addition to skeletal differences, recent American research suggests that women are more likely to suffer ACL injuries when they are ovulating, probably due to increased levels of oestrogen. The study found that there were five times the expected numbers of ACL injuries during ovulation and less than the expected number of injuries post-ovulation. This implies an association between ACL injuries and oestrogen concentration.

The female lower back is more vulnerable, too, because women, of the same height, have a relatively longer back than men, with a sacroiliac joint (at the base) that has a greater tendency to instability. This is particularly the case two days before and for the first two or three days of the period, and training should be modified accordingly.

CONTRACEPTIVE PILL USE

Taking the contraceptive pill regulates hormone levels, meaning that there are no hormonal peaks and troughs throughout the simulated cycle. This could possibly gain the athlete some protection against injury, the risk of which may increase at the point of ovulation in a normal cycle (see above). It will also mean that fluctuating hormones will not affect the favoured fuel source. However, there is not enough evidence at the moment (and it is not recommended) for the pill to be prescribed as a training aid.

TRAINING AND PREGNANCY

While high-intensity training will have to take a back seat for a while, you don't have to stop exercising through your pregnancy. However, it is important and sensible to get medical clearance beforehand and to follow the advice of your GP or midwife.

Exercise can be safe during pregnancy if modified accordingly and, indeed, offers some significant benefits:

- adaptation to changing body shape
- reduced blood pressure
- reduced fatigue
- possible reduced weight gain

- improved mood and self-image

- possible reduction in labour time

- improved endurance through labour

- reduced likelihood of caesarean

- promotes good circulation.

Here are some important guidelines to consider when continuing physical activity during pregnancy.

- **Don't overheat** – an internal temperature above 101°F can affect foetal development. Drink plenty of fluids while exercising and beware of exercising in hot weather. Wear loose-fitting clothing.

- **Don't overexert yourself** – this will prevent overheating as well as diminish the risk of you working too hard. You should not exercise to exhaustion or breathlessness.

- **Exercise should be light to moderate and aerobic in nature**. If using a heart rate monitor you may not be able to use the zones you used prior to pregnancy due to quite natural changes in your heart rate, but you should generally keep your heart rate below 140 bpm. It may be better to use rate of perceived exertion as a scale and only exercise at a 'comfortable' level.

- Remember that **relaxin** (a hormone produced during pregnancy) makes joints more lax and can increase risk of injury, so you should avoid running on uneven terrain.

- **If you don't feel like exercising then don't do it!** Nausea and other symptoms may physically prevent you from exercising anyway.

- **Now is not the time to worry about your figure**. Remember to account for your increased metabolic needs during pregnancy. Metabolism increases during pregnancy with the need for carbohydrate being the most dramatic increase. Pregnant women are at risk of developing hyperglycaemia, and insufficient nutrition will affect the foetus more than it will the mother. The general guideline is an additional 350 kcal per day, but you will need to account for any exercise that you do, too, and up your calorie intake accordingly.

POST-NATAL GUIDELINES

It probably isn't a good idea to set yourself strict time frames for your return to previous fitness levels as this may lead to you overdoing it and/or becoming disheartened. Everybody is different and there is no way of predicting how long it will take you to regain your form. Some people will regain their former fitness within six weeks but others may take six months.

Guidelines

- Start gradually and *only after getting medical clearance*.
- The first sessions should be easy walks of short duration.
- Gradually increase the duration of your walks and then start to include some brief intervals of jogging.
- Work up to half an hour of walk/run.
- Once you can comfortably achieve this four to five times per week, you should be OK to increase the pace slightly.

BREAST-FEEDING

Whether a mother is breast-feeding or not may affect her return to training – some women find it too painful to run if they are breast-feeding. Once again, the experience is totally individual: some women encounter rapid weight loss while breast-feeding, others find that they tend to store more body fat as a result. One thing to monitor is the baby's growth patterns. If they are insufficient then you could be training too much and may need to cut back. To ensure adequate milk production you need to make sure that you are consuming adequate carbohydrate and energy. There is also research that indicates that post-exercise breast milk will contain lactic acid and, while this is not harmful to babies, some develop a dislike for the taste!

Seniors

With increasing age comes a reduction in flexibility and a reduction in muscle mass. Both of these factors are reversible (to a degree) and both have direct relevance to physical performance and injury prevention.

Perhaps the most annoying aspects of growing older are:

- decreasing muscle mass (especially for women), so you get weaker

- associated reduction in the type of muscle fibres that provide speed, so you get slower, less explosive and less resilient (especially women)

- decreasing bone density – so that there is a greater likelihood of osteoporosis and bones are more easily fractured (sorry, but this too is more prevalent in women)

- an increased recovery time is required between any effort

- increased likelihood of a long-term health problem (for example, degenerating eyesight, dental problems, digestive upsets).

Right! That's the doom and gloom out of the way. Now for the good news ... How the body adapts to training is almost completely unaffected by age: you can start at 30, 40, 50, 60, 70, or whenever you want.

Fitness and exercise may not eliminate all the health problems listed above, but it can help you to recover from their effects and the effects of the treatments involved. However, there are some things that it is important to remember.

- **Use it or lose it!** Never give in and never stop taking *some* sweat-inducing exercise a *minimum of twice a week*. Because tennis demands agility, speed of movement, co-ordination, strength and general fitness, it is an excellent activity for seniors and an excellent activity for those who wish to stay fit.

- **Take care of your diet** – ensure variety, eat all food groups and look at Chapter 5 of this book, on diet and nutrition, to ensure that there are no deficiencies.

- **A health check** by a sports-sympathetic GP will ensure that you can start and/or continue your training with confidence.

- Cod liver oil and glucosamine supplements do help. (Again, see Chapter 5 – particularly the sections on diet and supplementation – for more information.)

1 BEFORE YOU START:
Your training toolkit

aim: to supply you with a set of tools and tactics that can be employed to help you set and attain your personal sporting goals, including:

- three basic 'ground rules' for success

- self-assessment tools

- details of how to achieve a solid base on which you can build.

Preparation and conditioning can and should be enjoyable and interesting; neither one need be a chore. A guide like the one you are holding can show you how to improve your training but this collection of paper, in itself, will do nothing for you. In order to get the most from this book there are three ground rules that must be observed, as outlined below.

Three important ground rules

Ground rule 1: honesty

Ever heard the expression 'In like a lion, out like a lamb'?

If you can be honest with yourself about what you want to achieve and what time you are prepared to invest then you have already taken a positive and one of the most important steps.

So, your first task is to evaluate *realistically* how much time you can spend and where it is going to come from. There is no point in setting unrealistic targets that are unachievable. The majority of us must balance work, social life and family commitments with training and playing. If you begin without thinking about a realistic balance then you will not stick to your programme. This is the road to guilt and disillusionment.

Recognise the following scenario?

Day one: 'Right! This is it – the big push for the new season. I'll get up at five every morning, run for an hour (that'll set me up for the day) and that'll leave the rest of the day free to plan my steamed fish and broccoli diet and my ten sessions at the gym ...'

Day two: [The alarm goes off at five] 'I'm a bit stiff after yesterday – best not do too much too soon. I'll skip the run and do double tomorrow ...'

By somewhere between days three and five you have talked yourself out of the early-morning run in the rain and by round about day six you are comfort-eating because you have let yourself down again ...

Never fear. You are not alone. Help is at hand.

The good news is that it is not impossible to achieve a sustainable balance and remain motivated. There are tricks that can be employed to help you, but from this point on you must be prepared to be brutally and consistently *honest* with yourself. If you are not prepared to do so then put this book down and get a beer out of the fridge – your interests lie elsewhere. And that really is OK – just don't kid yourself, or others, that you would do more 'if only ...'. That is just one short step away from 'You know, I could have gone all the way when I was younger ...', and there is at least one of those guys propping up the bar in every clubhouse, in every sport in the world.

Ground rule 2: pace yourself

Prepare to succeed. The first steps in any training programme are among the most important. Many people are put off even considering conditioning as a part of their tennis life because they wrongly believe it must hurt or is inherently boring. (But losing all the time hurts more!) The approach taken in this book is all about *planned progression*. It might not be original but it does work.

In brief: 'Try exercise A. When you can complete that, go to exercise B, which will be more intense' ... and so on. Not new and certainly no more than common sense, but so frequently ignored.

Some of the worst injuries treated at the Lilleshall Centre are directly attributable to shortcuts. A good example is athletes undergoing intensive plyometrics routines (see Chapter 3) when they have trouble supporting their own weight on one leg (this is no exaggeration)!

Just like a house, you will only be as good as your foundations. So although many of the exercises that follow may appear to you to be very low level and easy, *do not assume that they are beneath you* because, just like foundations, you skimp on them at your peril.

Consider the legend of Milo of Crotan, who lived in Ancient Greece (around 510 BC). As a young boy, on his way to the academy (where he studied under Pythagoras), he came across a baby bull calf. He was so taken with this animal that he picked it up to cuddle it and walked with it in his arms across the field. He continued to do this every day, progressing to carry it on his shoulders as it grew bigger, until eventually people would come from miles around to see the young man who could carry a fully grown bull.

He went on to win five consecutive Olympic gold medals in wrestling and there are many statues of him still around to this day.

This is a classic example of planned progression training: start small, form a base *with excellent technique* and what is built will be standing on solid foundations.

When we start to look at planning your training and objective setting you will see that we are developing a long-term strategy and that there can therefore be no shortcuts. But if you are clear about your destination and you have a 'map' to take you there (your plan), the steps along the way will be much easier to take.

From time to time you will still be feeling strong at the end of a session – the common mistake is to do just one more rep or lap and keep going until you reach absolute exhaustion. Don't punish yourself for feeling good – if you have planned to do five sets, do five sets – not six – just make a note in your diary and plan to do six next time. In this way you are constantly, but realistically, challenging yourself. You will soon find yourself eager to get back because there was a bit left in the tank last time.

Accepting this principle of planned progression is at the core of staying motivated.

Ground rule 3: quality before quantity. Always!

This applies equally if you are training on your own or in a group.

There are, unfortunately, many players, in many sports who consider that turning up is enough and that their own concentration, attitude and application are incidental. Any coach or guide can only set up an environment for practice. If the individual chooses to operate within that environment at less intensity or at lower quality than is required then it is a wasted exercise for everyone concerned.

To reiterate: this is the same whether you are training on your own or as part of a group. *You must concentrate on quality of exercise at all times.* Remember – clichés are sometimes where the truth lies:

Train hard, win easy

If you train at half pace you will play at half pace

But probably most true of all is:

Practice does not make perfect; it makes permanent

That is, if sloppiness is part of your training regime it will become ingrained in your performances.

Reminder

There are three ground rules.

1. **Honesty**: this is your tennis career (at whatever level) and the competition is ultimately with yourself.

2. **Pace yourself**: steady and consistent progression is the key; be patient – shortcuts lead straight to the physio's bench.

3. **Quality *always***: excellence is a habit and if it is the standard in your training then this can only have a positive effect on your game.

(Self-) motivation

If it was easy then you wouldn't have bought this book.

Motivational factors will be different for everyone. However, there are certain tricks and tactics that can help when the first pre-season flush of enthusiasm has waned and the alternatives to a cold, wet road or the gym are looking mighty warm and attractive. Read this section and think about how the points it makes might apply to you. Then try them out.

The keys to remaining motivated can be broken down into three distinct areas:

1. setting objectives

2. managing your time

3. measuring progress against your own plan.

With the correct approach, you can turn your own sports preparation into a project or hobby rather than a chore that has to be endured. After all, you aren't getting paid for it – it's OK to enjoy yourself!

Before you start you will need:

- a **stopwatch** (as cheap as you like)

- access to a **weights room** (don't worry if you don't have this – there are alternatives and we will look at those later)

- a **diary** (ideally one that has a page per day – it will be your record and your conscience).

top tip An ordinary hardback notebook will do as a training record but a diary is a thousand times better. The reason for this is simple – you only have one set of time so why have two diaries? Most people have one wallet because they have one lot of money! As your training must fit in with the rest of your life, a decent-sized, page-a-day diary will allow you to organise work, training records, social life and family commitments all in one place.

Objective setting

If you have no idea of where you want to go, how will you know when you get there?

Objectives – any objectives (be they work or play) – for you as an individual or for the group of which you are a part must follow some simple rules if they are to be effective. Effective objectives are often described as 'SMART'. This means they are always:

S – specific

M – measurable

A – achievable

R – realistic

T – timed.

It is perfectly acceptable to set an overall objective that is quite wide, but if you are serious about achieving a goal then you must follow the rules.

For example, a 'general' objective might be: 'I want to improve my speed.' It becomes a SMART objective when you say: 'Between the end of this season and the start of the next I want to be able to run 6 x 30-metre sprints, from a standing start, in under five seconds with a one and a half minute walk back between reps.'

S – specific: 'I want to improve my speed over short distances, e.g. 30 m.'

M – measurable: '... 6 x 30-metre sprints, each in under five seconds'.

A – achievable: e.g. 'I can currently do three reps without rest at this pace.'

R – realistic: i.e. the improvement is realistic (only you can tell this).

T – timed: 'Between the end of this season and the start of the next ...'.

An example of an un-SMART objective would be: 'I'm going to get myself really fit for next season.' It's non-specific, immeasurable, not timed and unlikely to be realistic. What does 'really fit' mean? How will you know if you have achieved your objective if you can't measure it and cannot specify exactly what you want to achieve?

You should also avoid negative targets, such as 'losing weight', as these are not tangible and it's therefore difficult to convince yourself that you have achieved anything. Figure out why you want to lose weight (or do you really mean fat?) and use that as the target – the loss of weight is a means to an end, not an end in itself. Please under no circumstances pin pictures of yourself looking fat on the beach last year to the inside of the biscuit barrel cupboard – this will merely ingrain a poor self-image. Much more effective are positive, dynamic, *focused* thoughts. Give yourself a break – you are human after all. Ditch the podgy photo and think out something more positive instead. An example might be: 'My target is to be able to achieve four miles inside 35 minutes while keeping my heart rate within "steady state". I will achieve this by 1 May.' The by-product of a large amount of steady-state training will be fat loss, if combined with the moderation of your diet (more on this later ...). As mentioned above, the fat loss becomes a means to an end rather than an end in itself – trust us, it's a heck of a lot easier that way.

The trick to major improvements is to break down the overall objective into smaller stages with short-term objectives. In this way you can see yourself progressing and you have more chance of staying motivated. These stages are best kept to two or three weeks at the most otherwise the target will seem too distant and disillusionment can easily set in.

When you set objectives plan to reward yourself when you achieve them (for instance, buy a special bottle of beer and keep it in the fridge ready for when you bench-press 90 kg for the first time or when you get under 30 minutes for that stamina run).

top tip When you are setting objectives that will run over a long period, measure the time in days rather than weeks or months: 90-day goals somehow sound a lot nearer than three months or 'in the next quarter'. And make sure you have an end date on which you will assess your success. If you set 90-day goals you can then break them into weekly and daily tasks.

Finally:

write the objectives down (in your diary) and tell someone close to you about them – it helps.

When seeking to set achievable goals it is very important that you assess where you are now and, consequently, what areas you need to work on. We'll look at how to measure your current strength, speed and flexibility later. From there you can build your own programme and objectives.

Time management

You can waste money, water, even breath – the only resource that can never be replaced is *time*.

Bearing in mind the life balance discussed earlier, time management is going to be the key to the sustainability of your programme. If you have set your short- and medium-term objectives but have been unrealistic about the time you can comfortably invest in them then your efforts are doomed before you start. *This is where personal honesty is the key.* The trick is to look at your current commitments and see where you can realistically grab time. The time you will need can be divided into two parts.

1. **Quality time**. This will be the one, two or three evenings a week that you spend at the gym, track or the club. In order to ensure that even these sessions do not become a burden, *plan your work*. For example, make sure that you plan your sets in the weights room, *before* you get there, then get in, do them and get out. Otherwise what should be a one-hour session can easily turn into a two-hour drudge and, before you know it, your evening is totally wrecked. Gyms are full of chatterboxes; be aware that you will reduce the effectiveness of the time you spend there by becoming one of them.

   If you have family or girlfriend/boyfriend commitments make sure that your partner is part of your planning process. It is no point planning to go to the gym only to find out that she/he-who-must-be-obeyed is going out and leaving you to baby-sit. Obvious, yes, but many people are sure to have been guilty of this in the past.

2. **Dead time**. This can be used as a supplement. Some examples of dead time and how it can be utilised are as follows.

- **Lunchtimes at work** – if you have a shower, how about getting out on the road? A half-hour run followed by a shower will still have you back at your desk/bench within the hour. No shower at work? Where is your nearest sports centre? They have showers.

- **While the kettle is boiling for your breakfast cuppa** – why not make it your routine to do a mini-circuit while you wait?

- **Him/Her Indoors left me to baby-sit** – get your 'Martini gym' out (all will be revealed later), do some skipping or try a mini-circuit.

top tip When you have identified your blocks of time, mark them out in your diary a week in advance (depending on how flexible your life needs to be) and then make a *timed* appointment with yourself and stick to it as strictly as you would an appointment with your boss. Planning on a weekly basis will help to avoid hijacking by unexpected events that may take precedence. Also, try to find a training partner who has similar commitments to you as this will aid your self-discipline.

Injuries – and how to deal with them

In the remainder of this first section we will be examining the ways that you can give yourself the best chance of avoiding injuries through steady, progressive training and correct technique. But, however well and carefully you prepare, you are going to pick up the odd gripe or twinge from time to time. Clearly in any sport this is inevitable so it is worthwhile knowing a bit more about the topic of sports injuries.

What are they?

Injuries come in many shapes and sizes. The blister that gives you a bit of a limp, the sprained ankle that keeps you out of action for a couple of weeks, and the completely torn knee ligaments that require major reconstructive surgery.

To help you to decide how to deal with the injuries that will inevitably occur through playing tennis, the following simple classification is a good starting point: *injuries are either due to trauma or to overuse.*

Traumatic injuries are easy to identify as there is a definite cause and effect (for example, falling over and twisting your knee). In contrast, overuse injuries are often difficult to diagnose and to treat. Traumatic and overuse injuries usually have one thing in common: pain. With traumatic injuries pain is usually acute and limits function (for example, the twisted knee makes you limp). Overuse injuries tend to give a more chronic, dull ache, which may come on during exercise but is often worse after activity and even at rest (night pain).

What pain can I train through and when should I just stop?

Pain is a warning sign of tissue injury and requires the modification of exercise and sport, or even complete rest. Minor pain and discomfort that doesn't get worse with exercise, and that gradually eases over a few days, indicates the presence of a minor problem. It may well be possible to play with such symptoms but the golden rule is that basic exercise function isn't impaired – that is, there is no visible effect on your sporting performance (such as a limp).

Irrespective of pain levels, *all* injuries to the head, neck and spine should be medically checked out (your union will have specific guidelines on head injury). The same goes for any high-speed impact injuries, particularly if significant swelling results.

First aid – what you can do yourself

RICE is an acronym that spells out a safe and effective remedy for all soft-tissue injuries. (An example of a soft tissue injury is a sprained ankle.) It is made up of the following components:

R = rest

I = ice

C = compression

E = elevation.

Rest

Don't do any more damage. Take complete rest ... that includes dancing!

Ice

The application of ice helps to reduce internal bleeding and relieve pain. Apply ice for 10-minute periods every two to three hours for the first 48 hours. Longer periods of ice application will actually accelerate the circulation, so don't overdo the timing.

Compression

This limits swelling and bruising. Make compression firm but not tight. Use crepe bandages or tubular elastic bandages. Make sure that circulation to the fingers and toes is not restricted by any compression bandages that are too tight.

Elevation

Reduces local blood pressure and helps reduce swelling. Keep the injured part higher than the level of the heart as this will reduce blood pressure at the site of the injury and help control swelling. So, for an ankle injury for example, raise the foot so that your 'toes are as high as your nose'.

RICE is the recipe of choice for the first 24–48 hours following an injury. If pain and swelling is not showing significant improvement after this period seek medical attention.

Rehabilitation

If you sustain a minor injury then a good place to start your rehabilitation is back at the simple tests that will be outlined in the following pages. These will test your flexibility and body weight control. If you can do these as well as you could prior to your injury then phase back gradually into light activity and short sessions until you have built up your ability to train normally again.

It is important that you are responsible and disciplined in your approach to injury management. Rushing back before you are ready will certainly leave you frustrated and can easily lead to further injuries. Bear in mind that if you have not been able to train for a significant period you will need to recover fully and then work back to *full* fitness to give yourself a fighting chance of avoiding further problems.

Eagerness to get back on the court following injury is totally understandable, but in retrospect it will seem ridiculous that you were not prepared to invest a couple more weeks to ensure 100 per cent recovery. It is hard, but try to be disciplined – you will thank yourself in the long term.

Where can I get advice?

If you have sustained a serious injury then it is essential to get a medical opinion (from your GP, club doctor or the local hospital). If you are not able to see a doctor then see a properly qualified (i.e. Chartered) physiotherapist who will help you to decide whether or not you need to see a doctor. (Look for the letters MCSP or SRP after their name; these stand for Member of the Chartered Society of Physiotherapy and State Registered Physiotherapist, respectively.) A physio will be able to guide you through your rehabilitation and get you back to playing fitness as quickly and as safely as possible.

2 BEGIN AT THE BEGINNING: PHYSICAL ASSESSMENT

aim:

- To enable you to assess your physical competence and make you more aware of any areas of weakness that need to be addressed.

- To give you an understanding of the methods that can be used to develop such areas.

Before you start

If you are motivated enough to buy this book in order to improve your game, you are probably already champing at the bit to get stuck in. *Hold your horses!* You do not have all the information yet.

You may be tempted to skim through the next few pages and feel that you know 'all that stuff' or that it is 'beneath you' – please assume nothing. By taking the time to read through everything in sequence you will, at worst, reconfirm the presence of your good habits and, more than likely, you will find that well-worn practice is not always the best practice.

As you read through, remember our three ground rules from Chapter 1:

1. **honesty** – there's no one else around to impress by cheating

2. **pace yourself** and build the intensity of your sessions gradually

3. **quality** – *always*.

This chapter has one more rule for you:

    4.   **variety** – keep varying your sessions.

It is easy to become bored with training (usually because it is carried out in isolation and is not part of a larger, longer-term plan). Remember that it's OK to enjoy yourself. Build up a repertoire of routines and rotate them to keep your training varied. Intersperse a hard session with a soft session, a hard week with a soft week, and so on.

Be creative. For example, if you are in a bit of a rut at the gym or on your stamina runs, then simply try combining the two every now and then. Perhaps find a wood to run through and there you will find logs to lift, (strong) branches to use for pull-ups, hills to sprint up, and so on.

Initial self-assessment

To get the most out of your training it is vital to know the point from which you are starting. With a fixed and measurable starting point you can target your efforts and gauge your progress.

Please do the tests that follow *in order* as they are, in themselves, progressive. If you cannot complete (*perfectly*) any of the tests you should see this as a warning that you have an area of weakness to address. If you skip any then you may end up on the physio's bench as you could be asking your body to compensate for a weakness you didn't know you had. For example, it is not uncommon for a bad back to be caused by all sorts of problems elsewhere: weak abdominals, one leg stronger than the other, and the like.

You wouldn't see a pilot take off without checking the aircraft over, so why wouldn't you take time to check yourself out properly? The areas you are going to check out now are:

- upper body (basic strength and stability tests)
- legs (basic strength and stability tests)
- abdominals (basic strength and stability tests).

Upper body strength and stability

Tennis requires good strength and control of your racquet arm if you are to perform well and avoid injury. It is important to check for some commonly encountered movement and strength disorders as the large amounts of repetitive force that tennis imparts upon the upper limbs can lead to injury problems.

The shoulder is a common site for injuries and pain in tennis players, with many injuries occurring because some muscles tend to get tight and strong while others become long and weak. A number of studies have shown that tennis players have a tendency to lose shoulder rotation flexibility. This is a key factor in developing pain as well as compromising power and technique. To get the best from your racquet arm the shoulder needs to be mobile, strong and balanced.

Flexibility test 1: pectoralis minor

1.

2.

How to do it

Lie on your back and see if the back of your shoulders is on the floor (picture 1). If not, see if you can push back your shoulders to reach the floor (picture 2).

Problems?

If you can't reach the floor with the back of your shoulders, practise the movement whenever you can by bracing your shoulders back as you stand or lie. Often just your racquet arm is tight while the other one is OK. It is important to try and improve this as tightness of this muscle will put the shoulder blade into a bad position, place extra pressure on the shoulder tendons and lead to pain.

Flexibility test 2: latissimus dorsi

How to do it
Lie on your back with your knees bent. Keep your back flat on the floor and raise one arm above your head, keeping the arm close to your head, until it rests on the floor.

Problems?
If keeping your back flat on the floor means you can't get your arm above your head to touch the floor then this could mean that the latissimus dorsi muscle is tight. This is a big strong muscle and if it is too tight this will affect how well the shoulder can move overhead. This could be linked with back or shoulder pain.

Tip
Ask a partner to place a hand under the small of your back at the start position. Try and press down on the hand throughout to keep your back flat to the floor.

Flexibility test 3: shoulder rotation

How to do it
Lie on your back with your knees bent and your arms out to the side at 90 degrees. Bend your elbows to 90 degrees and have your hands open/fingers pointing towards the ceiling. Turn your arms so that the backs of your hands and your lower arms touch the floor beside your head. This checks outward rotation of the shoulders.

Then from that position, rotate your arms as far as possible in the opposite direction without letting your shoulder blades raise from the floor. You should be able to get most of the way to the floor and both sides should be equal. This checks inward rotation.

Problems?

A loss of inward rotation is a common finding in most tennis players and is often linked with shoulder pain. Practise this stretch to improve the inward rotation, but if this provokes pain you should seek help from a qualified practitioner.

Stability test 1: repeated arm raises

This test is easier with a partner unless you have a room with 360 degree mirrors.

How to do it

This test is best done without a shirt on. Stand with your back to your partner and both arms down by your side. Get your partner to watch both of your shoulder blades while you lift both arms up and out to the side until your hands meet above your head. Repeat the movement five or six times. The shoulder blades should move smoothly and remain flat against the back as the movement occurs.

Problems?

If the shoulder blades 'come away' from the chest on the inner edge as in the picture (called winging) then the muscles controlling the shoulder blades are either weak or are not working at the right time to stabilise the shoulder. If this is the case then you should perform the shoulder stabilising exercises described later in this section.

Stability test 2: wall press-up

How to do it

Stand with your hands level with your shoulders and resting on the wall in front of you. Your feet should be slightly apart and about 30 cm from the wall. Keeping your body straight, drop your shoulders and push back away from the wall.

Problems?

If you are unable to push your body weight then there is gross weakness of the upper limbs. If the shoulder blades again 'come away' from the chest wall then this is another sign of weakness of the muscles around the shoulder blades. If you are unable to maintain a straight body position then the tests and exercises for trunk stability (see below) should be helpful.

Shoulder stabilising exercises

If the above stability tests reveal that you have any weakness then try to do these exercises regularly. Remember, little and often is much better than a lot all at once, and none of these exercises should be painful. Seek help if they are. If your shoulder blade control was poor, as demonstrated in stability tests 1 and 2, then practise exercises 1 and 2 before adding exercises 3 and 4.

Exercise 1

Stand with your back to a table or wall and your palm against it. Keeping your arm straight, push your hand in to the table – you should feel the muscles at the inner edge at the bottom of your shoulder blade working. Hold the position for 10 seconds, relax and repeat six times. Repeat as often as you can throughout the day.

Exercise 2

Stand upright with your elbows bent to 90 degrees. Brace both shoulder blades back and down as if trying to 'put your elbows into your back pockets'. Hold the position for 10 seconds, relax and repeat six times. Repeat as often as you can throughout the day.

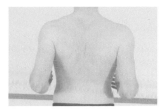 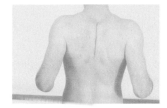

Exercise 3

While bracing your shoulder blades back and down, perform the wall press-up (see above). The 'bracing' action should keep the shoulder blade against the chest wall.

Exercise 4

While bracing your shoulder blades back and down, lift your arms from your side. Don't let your shoulder shrug up to your ear as you do this. By keeping the muscles working on the lower and inner part of the shoulder blade, the arm lifting should be smooth and should not cause the shoulder blade to come away from the chest wall.

Leg strength and stability

This section will look at how stable your legs are. This information is vital and, before embarking on any heavy strength work, it is important that you check out some basic body weight control movements. If your muscles struggle to control your own body weight then it makes no sense to load them with extra resistance in the form of free weights or machine weights.

It has been shown that in elite tennis players, only 30 per cent of the power needed for a serve is generated within the arm. The rest comes from the legs and trunk. This may not be the case for many club players either due to poor technique (see your coach) or to poor lower limb and trunk conditioning (look in the mirror). Here are some simple ways of assessing your lower limb strength and control. For adult players, any weaknesses that show up need to be addressed with a suitable strengthening programme.

For junior players the picture isn't as simple, as good control can be ruined by a growth spurt. This is because muscle flexibility and control may not keep pace with increases in bone growth.

top tip Check the height of junior players regularly so that you know if they are undergoing a growth spurt. If they are then training and playing times should be reduced as they will be at a greater risk of injury during these periods.

This is particularly important if you have suffered from a lower-limb injury in the past, which could have led to some muscle weakness or imbalance.

The three simple tests are:

- the side step
- the sit to stand
- the bum lift.

They will take you about 10 minutes in total but will save you a world of problems later as they will highlight any inherent weaknesses.

Side step

How to do it

Stand sideways on a bench that is around two-thirds of the height of your shin (measured while wearing your trainers). Keeping the heel of your test leg on the bench at all times, *slowly* lower the heel of your other foot to the floor. Touch the floor gently with your heel and return, slowly and smoothly, to the start position. You must keep the knee of your test leg in line with the middle of your test leg foot throughout. Repeat with the other leg and compare the two.

Problems?

The most common problem is a case of the wobbles: the knee of your test leg flicks from side to side, producing a jerky movement. Practise by dropping down to the point where you begin to lose control and then step back up. As your control improves you can step deeper.

The next most common fault is the knee of the test leg dropping inwards towards the other leg. If this isn't because your trainers have collapsed through years of overuse then it might be down to weak hip muscles; try the hip abductor test described at the end of this section.

Another common fault is an inability to retain control through the full range of movement. This is what is happening if you 'drop' the last two/three inches to the floor as your test leg fails. A good tip is to do the exercise to some suitably steady music, listen to the beat and use it to ensure that the full movement is done at a perfectly consistent pace.

Sit to stand

How to do it

Sit on a dining chair (with a maximum knee-bend angle of 90 degrees), with your arms folded, one foot flat on the floor and the other held up off the ground. Lean forwards and slowly stand up on your test leg (the one whose foot is touching the floor). Keep the knee of

your test leg over the foot throughout. Fully straighten the knee and then return slowly to the seated position. Repeat on the other leg and compare the two.

Problems?

Again the most common problem is the wobbles: the test leg knee jerks around uncontrollably. Try using a higher seat (or add cushions to raise the height). As your control improves you can revert to the original seat height.

As with the side-step test, you might find that the knee of your test leg drops inwards towards the other leg. Again, this could be down to weak hip muscles, so try the hip abductor test described at the end of this section.

Bum lift

How to do it

Lie flat on the floor with your hips and knees bent at 90 degrees. Place your arms across your chest and keep them there. Push down through both heels and lift your bum off the floor. You should aim to achieve a straight line between your shoulders, hips and knees. Don't arch your back when doing this. If you find it easy, then try the same exercise but just pushing down through one heel. Compare right to left sides. Are both just as easy or do you struggle to lift your backside with one side? Try 10 consecutive lifts with each leg. Just as easy? Or is one side quicker to fatigue than the other?

Problems?

You should not experience any back discomfort while doing this exercise. If you do it could be that you are not controlling your trunk very well. See the next section, on core stability. If one leg is weaker than the other, practise double-leg bum lifts, taking more weight on the weaker side.

Side lying abductors (hips) test

How to do it

Lie on your right side keeping your shoulders and hips in a straight line and using your right arm to prevent yourself from rolling forwards. Have both knees bent (as in the picture).

Keeping your ankles together, lift your top knee up towards the ceiling going as far as you can without rolling your trunk around at all. Control the knee back to the start position. If this is easy, try to repeat the exercise but this time keep the ankles just slightly apart.

Problems?

If you feel any effort in your back you are probably rolling around at the trunk, so keep your middle tight! If you find the movement is very jerky then you need to practise until it is easy and smooth.

Side lying adductors (groin) test

How to do it

Lie on your side with your top leg bent and your bottom leg straight. Use your forearm and free hand to stabilise your position (as in the picture). Try to lift your bottom leg, leading with your heel, keeping your leg in line with your body and keeping the knee straight. The movement should be smooth and controlled, and you should be able to lift the foot at least six inches from the ground.

Problems?

If you can't lift your leg at all, or can only do so by swinging the leg forwards, then your adductors are weak. This test can be used as an exercise to develop better control of this movement.

Trunk/core stability

If you haven't noticed, there are two major parts to your body: upper and lower. In many sports – and tennis is one of them – the power that is delivered by the upper body is to a large extent generated by the lower body (the legs). Unfortunately, the conduit of the power generated by these largest muscle groups is one of the most vulnerable sections: the abdomen, your mid-section.

Think of your abdomen as a corset of muscle that has four main sections: the front, the two sides and the back. These sections work together as a team and no one section should be emphasised above any other (although you are unlikely to get comments about your nice back muscles when you are on the beach …).

Bruce Lee was a great believer in the importance of the abdomen in the delivery of strength, and spent a long time working on it. This 'core' is seen as equally important today and the current vogue is for core stability training. This is nothing new, of course, but it's a great way to sell equipment to those seeking a shortcut. One of the current exercise fads is to use a big gym ball (or Swiss ball) to train the trunk muscles. Be careful when using these; remember ground rule 2: *pace yourself* – progress slowly and consistently. The aim of the gym ball is to destabilise the abdomen and, by putting it under stress, develop the supporting muscles. This is fine in theory but if you do not have a good basis of strength to start off with (your 'foundations'), you are heading for a fall.

There are a couple of simple tests you can do to assess how well your trunk muscles work as a team to support your spine. You should be able to do the following exercises well before contemplating the more demanding gym ball routines. Having said that, a good free weights programme together with sensible trunk conditioning work will significantly improve your core stability.

Finding your 'neutral spine' position

You will see the term 'neutral spine' used a lot in this book; it is an important concept as it is the best position for your back to receive weight. Concentrate on your position when you have completed the following exercise and remember it so that you can return to the same state at any time.

How to do it

Lie flat on your back with your knees bent and the soles of your feet on the floor. Place the palms of your hands flat on the floor, under the small of your back.

Push your back down towards the floor and on to your hands.

Arch your back away from your hands (keeping your bottom on the floor) so that the small of your back is now clear of your hands.

Relax again, so that your back is lightly touching your fingers, then take your hands out from under your back.

If you can do this in front of a mirror you will see a small space under your back.

In the following tests you should retain strict neutral spine position – whether flat on the floor or elevated from it. It is common for the space in the small of your back to collapse the moment your stomach muscles are employed. This is a classic sign of weakness.

> *It matters not a jot if you can do a thousand traditional sit-ups – if you cannot carry out these tests while retaining control of your spine you are building a house of straw.*

The principles set out here are frequently seen in Pilates classes, and it can benefit anyone who is serious about their sport to invest some time checking out a class or two.

Exercises

Leg bridging: stage one
How to do it

Lie flat on your back with your knees bent and the soles of your feet on the floor. Place your arms across your chest and push down through the soles of both feet. Lift your backside clear of the floor – high enough to make a straight line between the shoulders, hips and knees. Hold for a count of three, *with your spine in neutral position*, and then slowly return to the starting position.

If you are not sure that you have achieved neutral spine position then try doing the exercise in front of a mirror. If you do not have a floor-level mirror at home or at the gym, then you will find that patio doors work a treat. If you have no problems after 10 repetitions, go to stage two of this exercise (see below).

Problems?

The most common problem is poor control through the movement (i.e. failing to achieve a consistent speed throughout the movement and 'falling' through the last few inches). Rectify this by resting your arms on the floor at your sides; this will allow your arms to assist you. Once your control has improved go back to the arms-across-chest position.

Leg bridging: stage two

How to do it

As with stage one, lie flat on your back with your knees bent and the soles of your feet on the floor. Place your arms across your chest and push down through the soles of both feet. Lift your backside clear of the floor – high enough to form a straight line between the shoulders, hips and knees. Lift one foot off the floor. Keep your thighs parallel and fully straighten the knee of the lifted leg. The aim of the exercise is to keep your trunk and hips steady throughout. Imagine that you have a brimful pint pot sitting on each hip and, as you lift your leg, you mustn't spill a drop.

Problems?

The most common problem is a dropping of the hip on the side of the raised leg. Another problem is an excessive sway of the trunk and hips towards the supporting leg. Rectify this by placing your arms on the floor at your sides as this will allow your arms to assist your balance. Once your control has improved, go back to the arms-across-chest position.

Abdominal curl

How to do it

Lie flat on a firm surface with your hands on your thighs – in neutral spine position (see above). Sit up by curling your chin towards your chest, followed by your shoulder blades, then lifting your mid-back and finally your lower back from the floor. This must be done *slowly and smoothly*. Take at least four or five seconds to complete the movement.

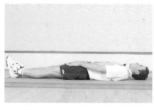

Keep your heels in contact with the ground throughout. It is vital to keep the lowest part of the back in contact with the floor until the rest of the trunk has been raised from the floor. If this exercise feels easy, try doing it with your arms folded across

your chest. Still easy? OK, then try it with your hands placed alongside your head (with your fingers outstretched and just touching your temples, not clasped behind your head or neck).

Problems?

The curled sit-up must be done smoothly. Any jerky movements indicate weakness or poor control. The early or mid parts of the curled sit-up are usually the places where difficulties arise. If you can't control the sit-up and do it smoothly and slowly, try the following. Start the sit-up from a semi-sitting position. This can be done by positioning your head, neck and shoulders against a wall, pillow or something similar. Practise the sit-up from this starting position and, as your control and strength improve, you can lower the starting point of the sit-up.

Back extension

How to do it

Lie flat on the floor, face down with your hands by your sides. Brace your shoulders back and lift your head and shoulders clear of the floor. Do this slowly with good control.

Problems?

Unable to clear your shoulders from the floor? This could be due to stiffness and/or weakness. If you can do a half press-up – that is, raise your shoulders off the floor using your hands (keeping your hips in contact with the floor) – then you have a weakness in your back muscles. If you can't, then the problem is one of stiffness. Doing half press-up exercises will help alleviate this.

Initial testing and ongoing measurement

If you can't measure it, you can't manage it.

If you've got this far without any ill effects you can (I hope) safely assume that you are not a complete physical basket case. The next step is to look at ways in which you can measure your own performance now and as you develop and progress.

Our team of sports scientists put professional athletes through such tests week in, week out. Usually, it takes us a week to complete a thorough assessment, but as you do not have the luxury of time, our years of experience have been compressed into a set of tests that you and your colleagues can complete in a matter of minutes. The results are just as robust and offer an excellent way to monitor progress and so help you stay motivated.

The key areas that we will now measure and assess are:

- explosive strength
- flat speed
- speed endurance (how long you can keep going at high speed)
- cardiovascular capacity (how long you can keep going at low intensity)
- flexibility (how bendy you are).

These tests have been selected and developed especially for the demands of your sport, which are extremely varied. So it doesn't matter what your best bench press is or how much weight you can squat with – you are doing this to improve your tennis playing ability. When asked what his bench press PB was, a GB champion shot putter was once heard to reply, '20 metres 85.' Get the point?

Don't mistake a means for an end, and remember those first two ground rules:

- pace yourself
- be honest.

It matters not a jot where you start with these tests – what we are seeking is *improvement* and *progression*. If you want to compare notes with a fellow training partner, then use 'percentage improvement' as your yardstick.

Tennis quadrathlon test

The first of these tests is called the 'quadrathlon'. It is easy to carry out and an excellent way of testing your overall fitness and progress. The test has four elements:

1. standing long jump
2. vertical jump
3. breeze-block drill
4. overhead shot throw.

It can be used to monitor your increases in power and, as it is a standardised test, you can use it to compare progress among your colleagues, providing a bit of friendly competition and so keeping things interesting. Record your times/distances on a record sheet so that you can monitor your progress.

Important

Only carry out these tests on a reasonably soft surface – definitely not tarmac or concrete. If you ignore this advice, you and your knees, hips and back will be very sorry, very quickly.

How to perform the test

Standing long jump

Start with your feet comfortably apart, with your toes just behind a take-off mark. Perform a single two-footed jump. Measure your longest distance. (Measure from the start line to the closest point of contact – i.e. if you fall backwards you mark where your backside/hand/ear touches and not your feet.)

Vertical jump

This test measures the difference between your standing reach and the height reached at the peak of a vertical jump. You will need to put some chalk on your fingertips to record your jump. Stand with your side towards a wall and reach up as high as possible with the arm nearest the wall, keeping your feet flat on the ground. Mark this with your chalky fingertips as your standing reach.

Now, standing slightly away from the wall, jump up as high as you can, using both arms and legs to assist. Touch the wall with your chalky fingertips at the highest point of the jump.

Calculate the height of the jump by subtracting your standing reach height from the jump height. The best of three attempts is recorded. Table 2.1 will give you an idea of how your performance rates.

TABLE 2.1 Vertical jump performance

Gender	Excellent	Above average	Average	Below average	Poor
Male	>65 cm	50–65 cm	40–49 cm	30–39 cm	<30 cm
Female	>58 cm	47–58 cm	36–46 cm	26–35 cm	<26 cm

Breeze-block drill

You will need a standard breeze block (cinder block) on its edge (i.e. with the holes facing upwards) or a gym bench.

Stand with your feet together, to one side of the block. With a partner to keep time and count, you should now jump, two-footed, over the block from side to side. Continue for 40 seconds, recording the number of jumps you do.

TABLE 2.2 Breeze-block drill performance

			Jumps		
Men	Women	Points	Men	Women	Points
100	95	15.0	79	74	9.0
97	92	14.3	76	71	7.5
94	89	13.5	73	68	6.0
91	86	12.8	70	65	4.5
88	83	12.0	67	62	3.0
85	80	11.3	64	59	1.5
82	77	10.5			

Overhead shot throw

Unless you have access to a 16 lb shot then it is DIY time. Lay your hands on a length of tyre inner tube, a bucket of sand and two heavy-duty cable ties (if you can't find

cable ties then use strong wire). Cut a length from the tube about two feet long. Use one of the cable ties to tie off one end. Fill the tube with sand until it weighs 7.26 kg/16 lb (or 4 kg/8.8 lb for women), then tie off the other end with the other cable tie. Hey presto! A home-made medicine ball/shot.

If you are unable to do this, simply find a lump of something that weighs 16 pounds: a log or a breeze block cut down will do fine. (You will have to do this test on grass, of course – the 'shot' will make a bit of a dent in the sward when it lands.)

Perform two repetitions only each side and note the aggregate distance (i.e. the sum of all throws divided by four). This is your score. Measure from the outside of the start line to the nearest point where the 'shot' touched the ground on landing. Check your score against those in the accompanying quadrathlon tables to see how you have done.

Quadrathlon tables

Points are allocated from quadrathlon tables (see Table 2.3) depending on the distance or time achieved. Scores are compared with the athlete's previous scores to determine the level of improvement. Competition should be based on the improvement on the previous test for each event, not on absolutes. Table 2.3 enables you to rate your performance in the standing long jump and the overhead shot throw.

TABLE 2.3 Test quadrathlon score table

Points	Standing jump	Overhead shot	Points	Standing jump	Overhead shot
1	1.00	4.00	51	2.06	12.50
2	1.02	4.17	52	2.39	12.75
3	1.05	4.34	53	2.41	12.92
4	1.08	4.51	54	2.44	13.10
5	1.10	4.68	55	2.47	13.27
6	1.13	4.85	56	2.50	13.44
7	1.16	5.03	57	2.52	13.61
8	1.19	5.20	58	2.55	13.78
9	1.21	5.37	59	2.58	13.95
10	1.24	5.54	60	2.60	14.13
11	1.27	5.71	61	2.63	14.30
12	1.30	5.88	62	2.66	14.47
13	1.32	6.06	63	2.69	14.64
14	1.35	6.23	64	2.71	14.81
15	1.38	6.40	65	2.74	14.98
16	1.40	6.57	66	2.77	15.16
17	1.43	6.74	67	2.80	15.33
18	1.46	6.91	68	2.82	15.50
19	1.49	7.09	69	2.85	15.67
20	1.51	7.26	70	2.88	15.84
21	1.54	7.43	71	2.90	16.02
22	1.57	7.60	72	2.93	16.19
23	1.60	7.77	73	2.96	16.36
24	1.62	7.94	74	2.99	16.53
25	1.65	8.12	75	3.01	16.70
26	1.68	8.29	76	3.04	16.87
27	1.70	8.46	77	3.07	17.12

TABLE 2.3 Test quadrathlon score table – continued

Points	Standing jump	Overhead shot	Points	Standing jump	Overhead shot
28	1.73	8.63	78	3.10	17.29
29	1.76	8.80	79	3.12	17.46
30	1.79	8.97	80	3.15	17.63
31	1.81	9.15	81	3.18	17.80
32	1.84	9.32	82	3.20	17.97
33	1.87	9.49	83	3.23	18.06
34	1.90	9.66	84	3.26	18.23
35	1.92	9.83	85	3.29	18.42
36	1.95	10.01	86	3.31	18.59
37	1.98	10.18	87	3.34	18.76
38	2.02	10.35	88	3.37	18.93
39	2.03	10.52	89	3.40	19.11
40	2.06	10.69	90	3.42	19.28
41	2.09	10.86	91	3.45	19.45
42	2.11	11.04	92	3.48	19.62
43	2.14	11.21	93	3.50	19.79
44	2.17	11.38	94	3.53	19.96
45	2.20	11.55	95	3.56	20.14
46	2.22	11.72	96	3.59	20.31
47	2.25	11.89	97	3.61	20.48
48	2.28	12.07	98	3.64	20.65
49	2.30	12.24	99	3.67	20.82
50	2.33	12.41	100	3.70	21.00

Measuring cardiovascular capacity

This is an area that can always be improved upon, and we will look in detail at improving and measuring your ability to keep going at low intensity for extended periods. On your progress sheet you need only record the duration of the exercise, which will increase week by week, as the intensity will remain constant.

The Harvard step test offers a good way to consistently gauge your level of cardiovascular (CV) capacity, and can be used in conjunction with the other tests described above to monitor your progress.

To undertake the Harvard step test you will need:

- a gym bench (45 cm high) – a beer crate is just as good
- a stopwatch
- an assistant.

The test is conducted by stepping up on to a standard gym bench once every two seconds until exhaustion, or for five minutes (150 steps) – whichever comes first. A single repetition is complete when both feet have returned to the start position. Note the following points.

- Have someone to help you keep to the required pace.
- One minute after finishing the test, take your pulse rate (beats per minute: bpm); record this as 'pulse 1'.
- Two minutes after finishing the test, take your pulse rate (bpm); record this as 'pulse 2'.
- Three minutes after finishing the test, take your pulse rate (bpm); record this as 'pulse 3'.
- Scoring: the score is equal to (100 x test duration in seconds) divided by 2 x (total heartbeats in the recovery periods). Don't worry if this doesn't seem very clear to start with – use the ready reckoner below to do the necessary calculations which will determine your level of fitness.

1. Duration of exercise: _____ seconds x 100 = _____
   - Pulse 1: _____ bpm
   - Pulse 2: _____ bpm
   - Pulse 3: _____ bpm
2. Add pulse counts 1–3 to get the total: _____ x 2 = _____

3. Divide the total of 1 by the total of 2 to get a total of _____
4. The total arrived at in 3 indicates a Harvard step test score of _____ (use the scale below to check what your score means).

A score of:

>90 = excellent
80–89 = good
65–79 = high average
55–64 = low average
<55 = poor.

Flexibility

To achieve your optimum level of speed, power and agility you must possess an adequate range of motion in, primarily, the shoulders, hips and ankles. Flexibility testing highlights areas of stiffness or tightness that can be worked on during your warm-down phase; this will reduce the chances of injury.

You can gauge your overall flexibility in under 10 minutes by carrying out the simple tests detailed below. If there are any of these tests that you can't do, concentrate on the weak area in question during your warm-*down* routine, not your warm-up (I will elaborate on this principle later).

None of the following tests provides any absolute measurements. They are valuable in that they offer a comparative measure that describes increases and improvements in flexibility.

Ankles

- Lie on your back with both legs extended and the backs of your heels on the floor.
- Point your toes as far away from you as possible – attempting to pass 45 degrees (i.e. halfway between the vertical and the floor).
- Compare the flexibility on each side.
- Now bring your toes back towards you as far as possible – attempting to pass the vertical the other way.
- Again, compare the flexibility on each side.

Elbows and wrists

- Spread out your fingers as wide as you can.
- Straighten your arm out in front of you, with the palm upwards.

You should be able to rotate your palm so that your little finger is higher than your thumb.

- Don't bend your fingers; keep them outstretched at all times. We are measuring the flexibility of your forearm not your fingers!
- Compare the flexibility on each side.

Groin

- While standing on one leg, raise the other leg out to the side.
- You are aiming to achieve an angle of 90 degrees between your legs.
- If you need to, you can hold on to something, or someone, to maintain balance.
- Ideally, stand with your back and heels against a wall. By keeping all your body in contact with the wall throughout, you will ensure that you don't cheat by leaning forwards or twisting your torso.
- Compare the flexibility on each side.

Hips

- Stand holding out a broomstick horizontally in front of you, one hand at each end, hands shoulder width apart.
- Without releasing your grip or moving your hands, bend down and step over the stick one leg at a time.
- Now step back through to return to the start position.
- Any acute inflexibility will mean you will not be able to complete this exercise.

Neck

- Normal flexibility will allow you to trap your flattened hand against your chest with your chin.

Shoulders

- In a standing position, attempt to clasp your hands behind your back by reaching behind your neck and downwards with one hand, and behind your back and upwards with the other.
- Try to link your fingers (or hands if you are more flexible).
- Repeat on the other side.
- Compare the flexibility on each side.

3 BEST PRACTICE

aim:

* To give you an overview of the key exercises and drills that you will be using in your training schedules.

This chapter contains all the elements that you will be using in your training schedules. Your objectives and how much you wish to commit to training will dictate which elements you will be using. However, do take the time to read through this chapter thoroughly and appreciate the need for quality at all times.

Warming-up and warming-down/stretching drills

Warming up and down will be a part of all training programmes, irrespective of your age, gender and objectives. Remember:

Weak and brittle things break.

Strength training on its own will address the 'weak' bit but ignore stretching and flexibility and you are just as likely to break down, as you will be too 'brittle' (i.e. not supple).

Contrary to traditional wisdom, a 'warm-up' is to prepare the body for exercise and it is not the best time to increase flexibility. Following exercise, the soft tissues will be warm and, as a result, their inherent ability to stretch will be increased. That's why attempts to increase basic flexibility should be made in the 'warm-down' period. For example, if you have one or two areas that you know are tight (hamstrings or calf, say), then it would be sensible to target these areas with stretches during your warm-down.

Warming up

The principle here is prepare the body for what you are about to do. Start gently and gradually increase the intensity to performance level. There are a number of benefits to warming up. A proper warm-up:

- can help prevent injuries
- facilitates the removal of any residual lactic acid from previous workouts
- increases the efficiency of contracting muscles
- enhances neuromuscular co-ordination (research suggests)
- increases heart rate and speeds blood circulation
- increases oxygen supply to the muscles.

Be careful not to warm up for too long, though, because you don't want to use up your energy warming up rather than getting an intense workout. You will need to sweat a little, but don't get fatigued by your warm-up. A good rule of thumb is to elevate your heart rate to between 120 and 140 bpm, sweat lightly, and have an elevated body temperature. Ten minutes' light running is a good way of getting your body warmed up.

If you are in the gym, perform one light set of each exercise and then gradually build up the weight. (Alternatively you can try decreasing time spent on the treadmill and building up time with a skipping rope – skipping is a great all-over warm-up exercise. Find a boxer and get him to show you some tricks to keep it interesting.)

top tip If you are going to skip, try to use a leather rope. It
turns more quickly. New ones can be broken in quickly if you remove
the leather, soak it for two days in water, dry it out and then leave it in
olive oil overnight. While the oil is still wet, hammer along the length of
the leather to break it in. Alternatively, you can use it for two years and
it will reach the same supple state about a week before it wears out ...

If you are on the track or on a court a good warm-up is a steady jog for about
half a mile (two laps of a 400 m track is OK) followed by some low-intensity
accelerations of, say, 50 m x 2 (jog into striding out, moving into three-quarter
pace, then back to jog), followed by stretching and drills.

Warming down and stretching

Chest

Sit on the floor, legs stretched out in front of you.
Rest your weight on your hands, which are resting
on the floor behind your back. Keeping your hands
where they are, and your arms straight, inch your
bottom forwards. You should feel your chest and
biceps stretch. If you do not, then return to the start
position and move your hands closer together. Keep
your chest puffed out and proud, to accentuate the stretch.

Triceps

Reach down behind your head with one
arm, as far down your back as you can.
With your free arm, *gently* push down on
the elbow to increase the stretch. Keep
your back and neck straight.

Back (upper)

Sit cross-legged on the floor. Reach forwards with both arms as far as you can. Relax your neck and keep your head up throughout the stretch. You will feel the centre of your upper back begin to stretch. Hold, and then reach over to your left as far as you can with your right hand; hold again, then repeat on the other side.

Back (lower)

Lie flat on your back with your arms out-stretched to each side, in a crucifix position. Bring your right knee up towards your chest and roll it over to your

left side, keeping your upper body still and your back still flat(tish) on the floor. Hold, and then change sides.

Abs

Lie face down on the floor in a press-up position. Keeping your hips in contact with the floor at all times, press up, arching your back.

Leaning your head back, look up as high as you can. You will feel your stomach muscles stretch. Push down with your hips to accentuate the stretch. To isolate the obliques (the muscles down the sides of the stomach) repeat as before, but look up and right as far as you can, then repeat looking to the left.

Neck

Sitting or standing upright, look over to your right as far as you can; try to put your chin on your shoulder. Slowly follow a semi-circular path down past your chest and up to the left, stretching all the time. Try to put your left ear on your left shoulder. Hold, then change sides.

Quadriceps

Standing on one leg, reach behind you and take hold of the non-standing foot. Pull gently towards your buttock (keeping a small gap between foot and bum) to stretch the front of the thigh. Keep your knees together and your thighs parallel. Maintain an upright 'running' posture throughout – do not lean forwards or to the side. Hold for 20 seconds on each leg and then repeat on each side, increasing the stretch.

Buttock and hamstring

Rest the leg you are stretching up on a bench, railing or the like. Ensure that you're standing leg stays straight at all times – drive back with your kneecap to lock this leg out. Push your hips in towards the bench in one smooth movement. You will feel the top of your hamstring and buttock stretch. (There will also be a secondary stretch to the standing quad.) Hold for about 30 seconds then repeat on the other leg.

Calf

Supporting your weight on a bar or bench, step back at least 1 m with one leg. Lock out this leg and, keeping that heel pressed into the ground, lean forwards to stretch your calf muscle, keeping your feet parallel – both sets of toes pointing forwards (as shown in the picture). Do not allow your front knee to bend too much – you should be able to

see the toes of your front foot at all times. Hold the stretch on each leg for about 30 seconds, leaning forwards slightly more as the muscle stretches. (To stretch the lower calf and Achilles heel, bend the back knee slightly but keep your back foot in contact with the ground at all times.)

Achilles

Leaning against a wall, support your weight on one leg while leaving the other out behind you, with the toe just behind the level of the standing foot. Push the rear foot flat on the floor and slowly bend the rear knee ensuring that the heel stays in contact with the ground at all times. Hold for about 30 seconds then repeat on the other leg.

Groin

Sit with the soles of your feet together, and your back upright. Press down gently on your knees with your elbows.

Hamstring

Lie on your back, keeping your right leg straight and on the floor. Pull your left knee to your chest, holding just behind your knee. Without letting your left knee move away from your chest, straighten out your left knee. You should feel your hamstring tighten as your leg straightens.

Glute

Lie on your back and cross one leg over the other. Pull the bottom leg towards your chest gently – you should feel a stretch in your buttock – you shouldn't feel uncomfortable at any point.

If you are unable to get into this position, just pull the knee to your chest without the leg crossed over and keep the other leg straight.

Strength training

Almost all players, irrespective of age and gender, will reap the benefits of resistance training. How it is used, however, will be dependent on a number of factors:

- younger players will be concentrating on strict form rather than heavy weights to ingrain good practice for later life

- players short on time will use it as part of a circuit training programme

- players seeking to extend themselves will need to focus on resistance training as a stand-alone training discipline in their schedule.

Strength training should be an important part of a tennis player's training repertoire. However, for many tennis players, even at the highest levels, resistance training has been noticeable by its absence. There have even been those who believe that training with weights will render the athlete 'muscle-bound'. Fortunately such views are becoming less and less common as there is absolutely no evidence to support them. (If you need a demonstration, then take a look at Olympic weight-lifters and the flexibility they require – bettered only by top-flight gymnasts.)

The overall aims of strength training are to improve a combination of performance and appearance. However, don't be shy about the importance of appearance – as long as it is viewed only as a by-product and not a goal to the exclusion of strength. It will make you feel better about yourself and you are likely to find that you will reach a stage when training is important to you because you like how you are starting to look and feel. Again it's that word honesty – we are all a little vain. (But don't kid yourself that you are going to have a washboard stomach without living like a monk. Be realistic about your objectives.)

As mentioned in the previous chapters, *planned progression is everything*. Hold that thought and not only will it keep you safe, it will keep you motivated too. This principle is particularly important when it comes to strength training. It does not matter what you can lift, it only matters that you become stronger than you are now, and thus improve your game, avoid injury and get progressively more satisfaction from the sport.

top tip Whatever else you do or don't do, remember to *keep a training diary*; record distance runs, sprints, every detail of your strength conditioning, games, your stretching and everything else. This will give you more motivation than a thousand psychologists! Be honest, accurate, detailed and up to date. If it isn't written down, it didn't happen!

A glossary of terms

Before we go any further, let us define some of the terms you will encounter that you may not have come across before. There will be others, but we'll explain those as we go along.

- **Aerobic exercise** – exercise in which muscles' demand for oxygen equals the body's ability to supply it.

- **Anaerobic exercise** – exercise in which muscles' demand for oxygen exceeds the body's ability to supply it; it produces quantities of lactic acid (the 'burn' you feel when a muscle exhausts).

- **Ballistic movement** – when the inertia of the weight takes over. Not good. Often encountered because the movement is too fast and uncontrolled. The official descriptions is: 'A fast, large-range movement that uses the momentum of a body part to exert an end-of-range stretch. Due to the speed and large amplitude of movement, this type of stretch is difficult to control and could cause injury.'

- **Compound exercise** – an exercise that employs a number of different muscles at once (e.g. bench press = chest and triceps).

- **Concentric** – the positive action when the muscle shortens under resistance (e.g. the up phase of a bench press).

- **Eccentric** – the negative phase when the muscle lengthens under resistance (e.g. the down phase of a bench press).

- **'Prime mover' exercise** – the opposite of a compound exercise; one that isolates one muscle group at a time (e.g. biceps curl).

- **Static or isometric** – when a muscle is under resistance but not moving (i.e. muscle contraction with no appreciable change in length). The classic example is to stand in a doorway and push out to the sides against the door frame with both hands. (Unless your name is Hercules or Samson, you are unlikely to move anything!)

Machines versus free weights

Are free weights better than machines? Well, it depends who you talk to. There is an argument to say that free weights offer a better simulation of real-life demands on your muscles; this is because the instability they provide recruits many stabilising muscles that don't operate during machine workouts. Anyway, here are the pros and cons so you can make up your own mind.

The advantages of machines

- They are great for beginners because they are safe and easy to use.

- Machines guide your body through a specific range of movement.

- You don't have to worry about balancing the weight as much as with free weights.

- Machines don't require as much co-ordination.

- Machines isolate each muscle group.

- Machines let you do a fast workout: you work your way through a circuit of machines and then, that's it, you're finished.

- Machines are usually arranged in sequence so that you work large muscle groups and then smaller muscle groups.

The disadvantages of machines

- Machines don't fit everybody. They can be hard to adjust.

- Machines don't build as much balance or co-ordination.

- Machines can force your body into an uncomfortable range of movement. (If you feel uncomfortable move on to another machine.)

- Machines are not portable. They can't be moved around very easily.

- Many trainers believe that working out with machines alone doesn't produce very effective results.

The advantages of free weights

- Free weights are versatile. One set of dumbbells can be used for many exercises.

- Free weights build better balance and co-ordination.

- Free weights work your muscles in a way that matches real-life demands.

- Free weights allow you to strengthen muscles and tendons that wouldn't get much work if you were using machines (i.e. the smaller, stabilising muscles).

The disadvantages of free weights

- Free weights can be difficult because of the balance and co-ordination required.

- A free weight workout will take longer than a machine workout.
- You can get injured more easily using free weights (if your technique is poor).

Spotting

If you are going to use free weights it will be difficult to ensure a really intense and safe programme unless you use a 'spotter' (someone who assists you in the ways listed below). If you train with a spotter or have been asked by a stranger at the gym to act as their spotter, there are some simple guidelines you should follow. It's a big responsibility for either party. Choose your spotter wisely and make sure that, if you are doing the spotting, you do so to the very best of your abilities.

- Pay attention to the person you are spotting at all times. Don't look at the totty/trouser across the room doing deep knee bends.
- Be prepared, instantly, to help the person you are spotting.
- Ask the person you are spotting if they would like you to put your hands on the bar/weights (some people like this and some don't).
- Ask the person you are spotting how many reps they think they can handle on their own.
- Make sure that you can handle the weight that the person you are spotting is using. If you don't think you can handle it, don't be macho and try to 'help' anyway.
- Offer only the effort the person you are spotting requires from you. Don't let the weight jerk around while they are trying to lift it, but never assist the last rep, and tell your spotter not to assist you. Make every rep an honest rep.
- Offer encouragement to the person you are spotting. This will really help them. With your encouragement, they might find they can squeeze out those last few reps.

Basic principles when training with weights

Remember, we are looking for weight training that mirrors what you do on the field. We want strength combined with speed. To achieve this, you must be strict about your form during exercise.

No doubt many players who have been working out for years know it all. However, there is always benefit to be derived from a coach reviewing form. Over time, you may slip into bad habits, so see this as an opportunity to go back to basics and check out your technique.

With all of the following exercises we are looking for the same basic technique strictly observed on every rep. Many bodybuilders will say 'the slower the better' – that's fine for the beach, but bear in mind that we are looking for the development of explosive power to put some pepper on that backhand.

For example, the bench press would be performed as follows.

1. Slowly down towards the chest (e.g. count of three).

2. The bar comes down slowly to lightly touch the chest.

3. Pause at the 'bottom' of the exercise (e.g. count 'one').

4. Power up – the bar is *driven* up powerfully.

Note: although *pushing* exercises like the bench press follow this pattern, *pulling* exercises follow the opposite path: that is, fast, powerful pull followed by a slow, controlled recovery to the start.

Breathing

With almost all exercises it is important to breathe out during the concentric phase and in on the eccentric.

Remember, the quality of the exercise, and therefore what you will get out of it, depends on retaining consistent, top-quality form throughout all exercises and all reps. One last poor-quality rep shouldn't – and mustn't – count.

> *Keep your form!*

Which weight?

Remember ground rule 2: pace yourself. There are no absolutes and it's only improvement that matters. (Milo was no mug – he started with a new-born calf!)

So be honest with yourself and use the correct weight for what you are doing. Of course, it should not be too light, but it definitely shouldn't be too heavy either. Don't be tempted to show off by 'going ballistic'. It is always more impressive to see someone who knows what they are doing rather than some idiot who thinks that the gym is the place for some sort of masculinity contest. Training in the gym should be done in a competitive atmosphere, but the competition is with yourself and your own development, not with the jerk in the flashy singlet (you can usually identify this guy by the fact that he has phantom lats and pretends his muscles are so huge that his arms cannot hang properly by his sides ... yeah right).

You will be surprised at the lack of weight needed to overload a muscle if you are *really* strict. (That sounds a bit like ground rule 3: quality before quantity – always!)

How many reps should you be doing?

> *I can't use weights – I don't want to end up like an East German shot putter ...!*

> *... but in my* Musclehead Monthly *magazine it says ...*

Let's get a few facts straight. What happens to your body during weight training depends largely on the amount that you lift and how many times you lift it. Individuals will vary but:

- **low repetitions** (5–8), heavy weight = no significant build-up of mass, big increases in strength and power

- **medium repetitions** (12–20), moderate weight = increase in muscle mass, slower increase in base strength
- **high repetitions** (20+), low weight = low increase in strength, benefits in local muscular endurance (fitness).

For the record: as women don't have the testosterone of a male player they will by nature find it more difficult to build muscle mass, but as a general rule – given that we don't want to be carting anything around a court that we don't have to – it would be sensible to avoid aiming to build muscle mass that isn't going to help you in your game.

If you are using weights in a stand-alone session in your week start with a weight that you can lift five but not eight times, build up to eight reps and then add weight:

Three sets of eight, up the weight!

If you are using weights as part of circuit training, and focusing on general fitness, then perform more repetitions with lighter weights.

Rest

Most people live very hectic lives and they don't get the rest or sleep they need. If you are training hard, you need to rest in order to recharge your batteries. You can't be at peak efficiency by staying up until one in the morning and getting up at six o'clock for days on end.

Over-training is not the preserve of elite athletes. The broad rules are:

- get 10 hours of sleep per night if you are a teenager
- get eight to nine hours of sleep per night if you are an adult
- schedule a 15-minute nap in the middle of the afternoon (most people can't do this, but if you are lucky enough to get the opportunity take it)
- keep vigorous activity to a minimum on your days off
- take a week off after six months of steady training.

Most of you will have to balance the demands of work, home, sport, family and so on, and will have to find a happy medium, but don't underestimate the importance of rest. In the right proportion it is as important as time in the gym or on the court.

Rest while you are working out is an important factor to monitor for two reasons. First, if you time your rest between sets and between exercises then you can slowly reduce it and so increase the intensity. Second, by keeping tabs on your rest periods you can keep your session moving along nicely. Also, when you put yourself under time restrictions you work more effectively and are less likely to get into a sloppy mindset, which is what I tend to do when I have no deadline.

Weight belts and straps

I have never seen anyone play tennis with a weight belt on ...

Many people work out with their weight belts permanently fastened. It's up to you, but all that is doing is ensuring that your lower back is not properly employed. This can easily lead to a weak back that needs protecting, and in this way, a vicious circle is set up. (Why people wear them to do biceps curls is a mystery! Maybe they think kit = proficiency.

Fact: lifters who use belts all the time have weaker backs and trunk muscles than lifters who don't.

If someone says, 'I've got a weak back so I have to protect it', the answer is 'Lose the belt, reduce the weight and sort out your technique.' However, if you are doing a heavy lifts session (see later sections) once in a while, then using a weight belt is a sensible precaution, but other than that I never wear one. In the end, though, it's up to you.

By the same token, try to limit the use of lifting wrist straps to exercises where you are limiting the stress that can be applied to a muscle group to the amount of strain the forearms can take. A good example is pull-ups where, on a final set, your back may still be going strong but you have exhausted your grip. At this point use straps to get that last set out. If you are going to use them, do so sparingly because (just as with belts) over-use will lead to weakness.

Essential exercises

What follows is a description of all the key exercises and how they should be performed. There are, literally, hundreds of different lifts with which any gym rat will bore you endlessly. Remember that we are looking for maximum effect for time invested. With this in mind, limit the exercises to those that provide the best overall returns. These are 'compound exercises' that employ more than one muscle at a time and, apart from being more time-effective, they replicate the demands of the game more closely.

The first set are the core exercises you will employ. You will notice that they deal with pushing and pulling in all three planes: overhead, in front and downwards.

Pay particular attention to how they should be performed as this will be very different from the slow, laborious way a bodybuilder would train. (Remember, 'train slow, play slow'.)

We will deal with the number of reps you need to do in a later section.

The exercises and programmes in this book are intended as a guide only and you should try to get a qualified coach to check you out on a reasonably regular basis.

Keep your form

At all times use a weight that will allow you to perform each exercise strictly, and then progress gradually to heavier weights.

With all dumbbell exercises, always start with your weaker arm/hand, first – that way you load each side equally and avoid imbalance injuries.

Alternate dumbbell press

Muscles employed: Shoulders, upper chest

Start position

Sitting, knees and ankles together, dumbbells resting on shoulders

How to do it

Drive dumbbells, one at a time, vertically

Try to ensure that the weights go straight up and down. Don't wander off at an angle. At the top of the movement, your elbow should be locked, with the weight directly above the shoulder. Lower steadily and repeat with the other arm. Begin the drive upward with one arm as the dumbbell begins its descent on the other. The dumbbells should pass at the top of head height. By sitting and keeping your knees together, your shoulders will be isolated more acutely. Keep your back straight – don't rock from side to side. If you cannot perform the exercise with perfect form then lose some of the weight and gradually build it back up again.

Pull-up (long arm)

Muscles employed: Back, biceps

Start position

On a chin-up bar, grasp the bar with your palms facing away from you, hands slightly more than shoulder width apart; hang so that your arms are locked out

How to do it

Pull yourself up so that your chin is above the bar, hold and then slowly return to the start position

Ensure that you lock out under control at the bottom of the exercise and don't 'bounce'. Try to keep your knees pointing at the ground and your feet up behind you

as this more accurately targets the muscles of the back. You will not be able to do too many of these, so on the last rep give yourself a boost up and lower as slowly as possible – this negative rep will eventually help you to achieve more full reps.

The above exercise is clearly dependent on your ability to pull up your own body weight. For most mere mortals this will have to be a target to work towards. If you are starting from a lower base then this same exercise can be used with much lower weights using a lat pull-down machine. The execution is exactly the same as above – just that the bar comes to you!

A further alternative for this pulling exercise is the prone pull-up. This can be performed in a Smith machine (where a 'captive' barbell is held in place on runners or chains) or even under a table!

Ensure that your body stays ramrod straight throughout, and does not sag or lag behind your arms.

Bench press

Muscles employed: Chest, triceps

Start position
Hands shoulder width apart on the bar (or holding dumbbells if you prefer); elbows locked out

How to do it
Steadily and keeping it under control, lower the bar to just touch the nipples; pause and then drive back up, keeping your elbows under the bar

There is a tendency to perform this exercise too far up the chest so that the bar starts above your nose and

comes down to your upper chest/throat. Without perfect form you will not affect the correct muscle groups of the chest. Think of driving the bar away from you rather than up and down.

The wider the grip, the more the chest is isolated. A narrower grip will isolate the triceps. This exercise can be performed with a barbell or dumbbells. *Always use a spotter for this exercise.*

Cheat one-hand row

Muscles employed: Back (lats, rhomboids), biceps, shoulder (posterior deltoids)

Start position

Kneel on a bench with your left knee and bend forwards so that your torso is parallel with the floor; your right foot should be standing on the floor, next to the bench, so that your legs are about shoulder width apart. Support yourself with your right hand on the end of the bench. Reach down with your left hand to pick up a dumbbell from in front of your right foot. The perfect position is with your spine in line with the bench, not angling off to one side.

How to do it

In one clean movement bring the weight straight up so that it is touching your chest between your nipple and your armpit.

Follow the movement through by rotating your back, and try to look up and behind you to ensure good rotation. Return the weight to the start position. It's a good idea to imagine that your spine is a hinge and the body is rotating around it, in this way you are using only the targeted muscles to move and control the weight. Ensure that the bench is high enough to require you to reach right down for the weight. This provides a rotational movement of the back muscles at the bottom and the top of the exercise.

Dips

Muscles employed: Triceps, lower chest

Start position

In a parallel dip rack, start with your arms at full extension

How to do it

Bend your arms slowly until your shoulders are as close to your hands as possible; pause, and then drive up hard to return to the start position

You can add weight by hanging weight discs from a belt with a chain looped through it. If you haven't got a dip rack then most squat/bench racks have handles on them for this exercise (see the illustrations). An alternative is to set up two benches in parallel; start with your feet up on one and your hands on the other, just behind your hips. Proceed as above. More weight can be added by resting weights in your lap. Weight can be reduced by performing the dip from a bench (as shown in the pictures).

Upright row

Muscles employed: Back (lats, rhomboids), biceps, shoulder (anterior deltoids)

Start position

Stand (back straight, looking straight ahead) holding a barbell, which should be touching your hips, your arms locked out and legs slightly bent to reduce any strain on the lower back; your hands should be close together on the bar (about two thumb lengths apart)

How to do it

Pull the bar up to your chin, keeping your elbows as high as possible; pause at the top and then lower slowly to the start position

Do not drop the bar through the last few inches as this is a great way to damage you shoulders and back. Keep the bar under control at all times. The closer together your hands, the more acutely the exercise isolates your shoulders.

Side bends

Muscles employed: Back (lats), sides (obliques), abdominal muscles

Start position

Back straight, feet slightly wider than shoulder width apart, holding a dumbbell in each hand, one against the outside of each leg

How to do it

Lower the right-hand weight down the line of your right leg as far as it will go; pause, and then bring it back to the start, continuing through to lean over to your left side, repeating the along-the-leg movement

Ensure that you do not lean forwards during the exercise as this transfers any stress to your back.

Lower body strength training

Later on you will see some schedules that feature Olympic lifts, which offer a much more dynamic leg workout than squats alone. They demand co-ordination as well as strength and therefore take some mastering, but *don't use this as an excuse to miss them out.*

Squat routines

There is always a temptation to omit squats from training routines. There is a reason for this. There is a tendency for people to perform these exercises badly, which then puts massive strain on the knees and back – not good. Also, it tends to be a very slow exercise, which does nothing for the dynamic power a tennis player needs. However, if performed accurately and starting with a low weight to perfect technique, squats can add great value to your training.

Safety considerations for the squat

Keep your chest high, head up and back flat throughout. Use manageable loads until your technique is perfect and *ingrained*! Use spotters or a squat rack; *never* squat down on to a bench – one heavy sit-down and you'll have destroyed your vertebral discs! Use either full or half squats in a session, not both. You may use light jump squats after either full or half squats for a very dynamic, demanding workout for the legs.

HALF SQUAT

This is a core-vital exercise for everyone, and everyone can do it – even if only with a broom handle. It targets the hip and leg extensors and all trunk muscles, which are used to maintain correct posture.

Face the squat rack, on which the bar should be at just below shoulder height. Take the bar on your shoulders, stand up and take a step back. Keep your feet flat on the floor, just over hip width apart, toes pointing slightly outwards.

Breathe in and bend your knees until your thighs are at an angle of 45 degrees to the ground. Keep your back flat and vertical; hold for a moment, then, breathing out, powerfully straighten your legs and push your hips forwards until you are upright. *Do not 'snap' your knees back at the top of this exercise as this can over-extend the joint and cause injury.*

FRONT SQUAT

You will be surprised at how much this targets the muscles of the trunk as well as the legs and backside.

Face the rack, on which bar should be just below shoulder height. Take the bar on the front of your shoulders/top of your chest. Stand up and take a step back. Keep your feet flat on the floor, just over hip width apart, toes pointing slightly outwards.

Breathe in and bend your knees until your thighs are parallel to the ground. Keep your back flat and vertical; hold for a moment, then, breathing out, powerfully straighten your legs and push your hips forwards until you are upright.

It is very important that you keep your chest high throughout to ensure that the weight is transferred straight down through your heels.

If you struggle with the shoulder flexibility required to hold the bar in the 'clean' position, then cross your arms over the bar as pictured and this will secure it in place. (However, if you cannot hold the bar in 'clean' then this is an indicator that you should be working on your shoulder flexibility – see the advice on this in Chapter 2.)

JUMP SQUAT

A great power and speed developer and, again, even if you start out using just a broom handle it is a core-vital exercise.

Follow the starting and safety procedures as for the half squat, but there should be less of a knee-bend and much less weight used than in that exercise. When in your lowest position jump vertically upwards and, on landing, rebound. Keep your back flat, your head up and your body vertical. Note that you should keep your knees bent to cushion your landing.

STAR SQUAT

Another exercise that is a great power and speed developer.

Follow the starting and safety procedures as for the half squat. With the bar on your shoulders, step out to your right half a stride, do a half squat and then return to the feet-together position. Repeat on the left side, to the front (on both right and left leg) and finally take a half stride back with each leg. Essentially, this is a lunge to all points of the compass.

A word of caution: even for advanced trainers a reverse lunge can feel very unusual and unstable so always start with very low weight with which you feel confident and then build up gradually.

Olympic lifting technique

Why lifts?

Olympic lifts use more muscle groups and more muscle mass in complex movement than any other movement or exercise – and they use them *fast*, unlike power lifting (bench presses, squats and dead lifts). This means that you train speed, co-ordination and explosive strength, right from the early stages. Look at the photos in this section and see for yourself!

These exercises are suitable for all groups provided there is a concentration on form and technique over gross weight. Lifters take a lifetime (literally) to perfect technique and age is no barrier to starting: I started lifting at 36 and there is a world 'Masters' circuit that includes people of 80 years plus).

Simple precautions

You will need sturdy supportive footwear, not beat-up old trainers! You will also need an uncluttered area for lifting, with a non-slip floor. Use Olympic (20 kg) bars whenever possible – they have revolving sleeves and allow the hands to flip or rotate without the mass of the discs causing the bar to twist, which might result in breaking your grip or damaging your wrists.

Each exercise is accompanied by illustrations to help demonstrate the basics of the techniques required. Start off with light weights and concentrate on technique, building up gradually. Because form and technique are so vital, it is a good idea to train with a partner so you can check each other out as you go. If you have an experienced lifter at your gym who can review your lifts periodically, so much the better.

You are strongly advised not to max out on any of these lifts without proper tuition, supervision and practice. You will get plenty of benefit from using lighter weights and strict form on each rep.

top tip Olympic weights are all nine inches in radius because this is a safe height from which to begin lifts. Starting any lower (i.e. with smaller-diameter discs) would put unnecessary strain on your back and knees. Most gymnasiums only have nine-inch-radius weights, starting at 20 kg, including a bar (an Olympic bar is 20 kg) that is a minimum of 60 kg – a bit too heavy for practising complex lifts. You can get round this problem by building some wooden dummy weights. Cut two nine-inch-radius discs out of plywood or MDF and put holes in the centre to fit your barbell. This means that you can practise the movements in safety – without any weights at all, perhaps – and build up gradually by adding small weights to the dummies. You can do the same with one-inch-diameter bars.

One-hand snatch

This is the safest, most dynamic, most important, relevant lift of all, the one-hand snatch will strengthen quadriceps, hip extensors, lower back, hamstrings and backside, calf muscles, upper back, shoulders, back, biceps, chest and triceps – and give a great plyometric workout to the whole body as the dumbbell is 'caught' overhead. It will also greatly improve trunk stability as one side of the body works and the other stabilises. It is an exercise where, even if technique is not perfect, maximum effort can be made.

Remember, there are few human movements where the muscular effort is equal on both sides of the body: we run left, right, left, right, and serve with one limb at a time, so the one-hand snatch is most appropriate as a training exercise.

Note that the path of the dumbbell is perfectly vertical throughout this lift.

GET SET

Start with your feet just over hip width apart. Your back should be flat and your shoulders just over the weight. The dumbbell should be on the floor parallel to

your shoulders and between your feet; one hand should over-grip the dumbbell with your knuckles facing forwards. Keep your head up, looking forwards. Keep your lifting arm relaxed but with some pull on the dumbbell (so that there is no slack that will allow you to 'jerk' and jar your shoulder muscles) Your free hand should rest on your thigh, just above knee.

FIRST PULL

Ease the weight off the floor (no jerking!) by driving through your heels and, as the weight passes your shins, push down hard on your thigh with your free hand to give extra acceleration. Keep your lifting arm straight, and keep accelerating dumbbell. When the dumbbell is level with your groin, move on to the ...

SECOND PULL

Keep accelerating the weight, rise on to your toes, raise (shrug) your shoulder and fully extend your body. Now move into the ...

THIRD PULL

(The weight should be moving at its fastest now.) Keeping the weight close to

your body, continue to lift by pulling upwards until your upper arm is close to your ear and the weight is at chest height. Then ...

CATCH

At this point stop pulling and, very quickly, dip (by bending your knees, jumping your feet a few centimetres further apart and pushing yourself down by pushing upwards on the dumbbell), flip the wrist to knuckles-back position and 'catch' the weight at arm's length overhead. Hold this receiving position for two seconds.

RECOVERY

Straighten up, bring your feet together, hold the final position for two seconds, then lower the weight to your shoulders (using both hands), then your thighs, then lower to the floor, smoothly, by bending your knees and keeping your back flat.

Repeat with your other hand.

The power clean and jerk

This is an important power exercise for development of the leg and hip extensors, lower back, trunk stabilisers, deltoids, trapezius and shoulders generally; it will also develop co-ordination and timing, and the catch (when done properly) gives a strong plyometric stimulus to the whole body.

> *Remember that good technique is essential – not only for biomechanical efficiency but for your safety too. Quality always!*

GET SET
Start as for the snatch, above, but with your hands only fractionally wider than shoulder width apart.

FIRST PULL
Lift the bar by gradually straightening your knees. Keep your head up and your back flat. *Do not jerk at the bar or bend your back*, your arms should still be taut like cables. Keep the bar close to your shins.

SECOND PULL
Rise on to your toes, raise (shrug) your lifting shoulder and fully extend your body. This pull moves into third pull when your hips thrust forwards and the bar brushes your thighs just above the knees.

THIRD PULL
Keep the bar accelerating by shrugging your shoulders and, keeping the bar close to your body, driving your legs vertically and rising on to your toes. Now add height to the bar by pulling upwards with your arms, by bending our elbows outwards, then move on to ...

CATCH

When the bar reaches nipple height, quickly bend your knees, jump your feet a few centimetres farther apart and drop under the bar, catching it on your deltoids with your elbows high. Hold for a second and then ...

RECOVERY

Straighten your legs, stand up, bring your feet back to the starting position, keeping your elbows high, and get ready to perform the *jerk*.

DIP

Keep the bar on your front deltoids and your elbows *very* high (see photo), keep your feet flat, bend your knees slightly and, with no delay, go into ...

DRIVE

Drive up vertically with all your speed and strength so that you force the bar to above head height.

SPLIT

As the bar passes your eyes, push yourself under it by splitting your legs as shown in the photo (do not jump up) so that the bar is at arm's length overhead. Hold for a second or

two. (Study the photo: during this split stance, split your feet to at least one and a half times shoulder width, keeping your rear heel in line with your calf, your front foot turned slightly inwards for stability.)

RECOVERY

Half step back with your *front* foot first – *this is a vital safety precaution*. Recover your back foot so that the feet are together, then return safely to the floor

Repeat the lift, alternating feet during the split stance so that equal training is given to both sides.

Trunk exercises

As a starting point you will have performed all the tests in Chapter 2, which will give you a pretty good idea of how stable you core is. (The current fashion is to describe such routines as 'core stability' exercises, and use all sorts of big rubber balls and wobbly boards to destabilise the trunk while exercising.) One word of warning, though: unless you have (a) performed all the tests in Chapter 2 perfectly and (b) have the following exercises under control, then using gym balls (Swiss balls) can cause problems. It's a bit like trying to ride a unicycle if you haven't even got the hang of your trike. Think back to the legend of Milo and his calf again.

Slow crunches

We will call this a sit-up but, strictly speaking, it isn't.

Start position

Lie flat on your back with a *neutral spine*, feet flat on the floor, knees bent. Place your hands on your thighs – arms straight.

How to do it

Breathe out and pull your navel in towards your spine. This will brace your muscles. Now concentrate on using *only the muscles in your stomach* to curl your shoulders off the floor. Slide your hands

along your thighs until your shoulders are clear of
the floor; hold for a good second and then return,
slowly, to the start. This is one repetition.

The movement that you are looking for is a curl
and not really a sit-up at all. This is a very subtle,
slow and steady movement – even tempo, up and
down – controlled throughout.

Lying sides

Start position
Lie on one side, top arm lying along your top side. Your back, chest and legs
should remain in a straight line throughout.

How to do it
Breathe out and pull your navel towards your spine.
This will brace your muscles. Now concentrate on
using *only the muscles in your side* (the side that is
'on top') to lift your legs clear of the floor; hold for a
good second and then return, slowly, to the start.
This is one repetition.

Concentrate on keeping your body straight throughout. Imagine that you are
being squeezed between two boards, in front and behind, so your body and legs
cannot move forwards or back, only up and down. If, after about eight repetitions,
you cannot feel your obliques (sides) working then you are probably not
performing this exercise correctly.

Bridge

Start position
Lie flat on the floor with your heels flat on the floor and your arms across your
chest. Push down through both heels and lift your bum off the floor. Aim to achieve
a straight line between your shoulders, hips and knees. Don't arch your back
when doing this.

How to do it
Pushing down through one leg, lift the other off the floor and reach out and point
with your toes. Your pointing leg should be parallel to the ground and not pointing

up in the air. Return to the start, *under control*, and repeat on the other side.

There must be no dipping or rotating of the hips during the exercise.

For advanced athletes only: rest a weight disc on your stomach during the exercise.

Plank

Start position

Rest your weight on your elbows rather than your hands. Concentrate on ensuring that your back and legs are in a straight line (see below).

How to do it

Start the exercise by bracing your abs and back – breathe out and then *slowly* raise your right leg while keeping it straight until your thigh is parallel to the floor. Hold and then return, slowly, to the starting position.

If your back sags or your pelvis twists during the exercise then this does not count. *Only strict form counts!*

When you have performed one on either side this is a single repetition.

Superman

This is a progression of the plank.

Start position

Start in a bridge position, torso and legs in a straight line, pelvis parallel to the floor.

How to do it

Raise your left leg (as per the plank, above) and reach out with your right arm until both leg and arm are parallel with the floor.

Try to keep your spine in the neutral position at all times and do not let your pelvis tilt. Once each side = one repetition.

Chinnies

Start position

Lie flat on your back with your legs out straight. Your fingers should be touching your temples, elbows out to the side (you should *not* have your hands clasped behind your head, as this encourages the tendency to jerk the head and lift from the neck.)

How to do it

Pull your left knee towards your right elbow, at the same time sitting up to bring that elbow to your left knee; lie back, touch both elbows to the floor again, driving your left leg out straight as you do so. Then do the same with the right knee and the left elbow.

Once you have got the hang of the movement, speed it up. This is a speed exercise.

Advanced trunk exercises

Advanced reverse crunches

You will need a partner for this one.

Start position

Lie flat on your back with your partner standing astride your head. Take hold of his/her ankles. Ask your partner to hold their hands out straight in front at shoulder height with their palms facing down. Keeping your legs straight, raise your feet about 5 cm. This is your start position.

How to do it

Now, in one smooth movement, bring your legs to a vertical position (no further), reach up with your feet and touch your partner's hands. Slowly and smoothly return to the start position.

This exercise only works if you keep your legs straight and do not stray over the vertical. Anything other than *strict form* is a waste of time.

As a progression you can do small circuits and pyramids – reach up and touch once and then, without lowering, touch twice, three times, twice, once, and so on.

The 'Martini gym'

It's honesty time again ...

You've all heard most of the classic excuses ('I already know what I should be doing but I haven't got the time or money to invest in joining a gym' and such like). If there are any genuine problems, then there are usually ways around them. Of course they will only be effective if you genuinely want to train and aren't covering up the fact that you just can't be bothered.

In order to maintain muscle strength and mass you have to work out at least once a week, twice if you want to make gains, and for tennis players a maximum of three times a week. This obviously presents a problem for those who have limited time at their disposal. Never fear – all is not lost.

You can establish a perfectly good gym at home: the 'Martini gym' (so-called because, like the drink of that name, it can be used 'any time, any place, anywhere'). It will cost you nothing and, as you can use it without leaving home, it has a double benefit. You can have a workout and be in the shower inside an hour. You can even do it while baby-sitting: exercise and brownie points!

Even if you can only grab half an hour three times a week, that's enough to maintain upper body muscle fitness. If you can schedule yourself two one-hour sessions then you're laughing.

Here's how. Table 3.1 lists the key exercises and gives details of how you can improvise. If the kit specified doesn't quite work for you, then adapt it or change it, but don't use it as an excuse to do nothing. *Remember, be honest ...*

Shopping list

You will need a bit of kit to do the following 'Martini gym' workouts, but it can all be scavenged or found at car boot sales.

- 25 kg of sand
- 12 x 'common' house bricks
- 1 x old backpack or sports bag
- 1 x old small suitcase or hard briefcase
- 1 x bin liner
- 1 m rope (enough to take your body weight)
- 1 x bathroom scales

Everything else listed in Table 3.1 can be found in or around the house.

TABLE 3.1 The 'Martini gym' home workout

Exercise	Kit	Method	Tips	To make it harder
Bench press	3 x *sturdy* dining chairs bin liner sports bag or backpack bricks, stones or sand for weight	Feet on one chair and hands on the other two, a little wider than shoulder width apart. Keep your body in a straight line – head, back, legs – and lower until your thumbs are parallel with your armpits, then push up	Be strict. Move down slowly and as deep as you can; hold for a split second, then up hard and fast. Concentrate on your form: keep your body in line and don't be tempted to rush or 'bounce' off the bottom of the exercise. If you want an incline press, simply elevate your feet.	A bin liner filled with stones or sand, placed in a rucksack and worn or resting between your shoulder blades will add more weight. (You won't need much – if you weigh 13.5 stones then you are already pressing around 70 kg using just your body weight.)
Pull-ups	1 x *sturdy* table or adjustable chin-up bar (available from most Argos-type catalogues or sports shops)	Lie on your back with your feet under the table. Reach up with your hands as wide as possible, hold on to the edge of the table (or the chin-up bar) and pull up until your chest meets the underside of the table. (Ideally, you should start with your hands one and a half times shoulder width apart, palms facing towards your feet.) You should pull so that your nipples stay on the same plane as your hands. Follow the same form as you would with a strict press-up: keep everything in line – head, chest, legs, etc.	You can vary the weight by bending your knees and moving your feet back towards your backside. The further away from your hands your feet are, the harder it is. Be strict: just because you are bending your legs there is no excuse to let your body sag.	Elevate your feet on a stool or a chair. (Obviously you can't go higher than the underside of the table, but that will be plenty and if it isn't then add some weight to your lap – but *keep your form!* Never sacrifice form for weight.)

TABLE 3.1 The 'Martini gym' home workout – continued

Exercise	Kit	Method	Tips	To make it harder
One-hand row	1 x builder's bucket, or suitcase bricks, stones or sand for weight 2 x *sturdy* chairs 1 x length of rope	Place the chairs side by side (to form a makeshift bench) and rest your left knee and left hand on them. Reach down with your right hand to pick up the bucket and pull until your hand is level with your armpit. Continue the movement through by rotating your back to lift that few extra inches, then reverse the movement slowly.	You must ensure that you really have to reach down at the start of the exercise. This may mean that you have to elevate your stance – maybe you could use a workmate instead of the chairs? You may have to use the rope to get the full range. You will have to shorten it, of course, but just double it round to save cutting it.	Put more in the bucket dear Liza, dear Liza . . .
Upright row	1 x builder's bucket, or suitcase bricks, stones or sand for weight 1 x length of rope (about 1 m)	Stand up, with a straight back, looking straight ahead, with the bucket held in both hands, arms fully extended downwards. Pull up in one smooth action, keeping your elbows high, until your knuckles touch (or almost touch) your chin; hold, then release slowly to full extension.	Keep your elbows high and hold for a moment at the top of the exercise to squeeze those shoulders. Concentrate on form; it is all too easy to get lazy and shorten the range of movement or start leaning forwards and jerking the weight up. If this happens, lose some of the weight.	Put more weight in the bucket.

Exercise	Equipment	Technique	Tips
Overhead press	1 x wall	Kneel down, ankles together, with the soles of your feet pressed against the bottom of the wall. Put your hands on the floor, thumbs together, about a foot in front of your knees. Put your head on the floor between your index fingers. Keeping your hands, feet and head where they are, straighten your legs. Your body weight is now directly over your hands – straighten your arms to perform an overhead press.	Be strict: down slowly, hold for a split second, then up hard and fast. If you are struggling with the weight, move your hands forwards, away from your knees, and the weight will reduce. You can also widen the space between your hands to reduce the weight.	The closer your hands are to your knees, the heavier the weight. To keep a record of your progress, measure how far your hands are from your knees; you can progress in stages by moving your hands one inch closer to your knees.
Dips	3 x sturdy dining chairs, bin liner sports bag or backpack bricks, stones or sand for weight	Set up the chairs as for the bench press: feet up on one chair, hands just to the sides and rear of your hips on the other two. Dip as low as possible – slowly; hold, then drive up to full extension, hard and fast. Hold again, then repeat.	Concentrate on form and getting full extension on every rep.	Use a backpack or bag filled with a bin liner of stones or sand to add weight (as for the bench press), but this time rest the weight in your lap. Remember to measure the weight used and record your progress. Alternatively, the corner where two parts of the kitchen work surface meet at a right angle makes a great dip rack.

If you are struggling with the bucket try to get hold of an old briefcase or suitcase and use that instead. Because it is slimmer, this means that your hand will stay closer to your body during the lifts, which you may find easier. If you are not a fan of physical comedy, an old belt or rope will ensure that it doesn't fall open unexpectedly.

Medicine ball work

Mark Twain once said 'Learn to ride a bicycle – you will not regret it if you live.' He may or may not have been right about the bicycle, but what he said certainly applies to the medicine ball!

Medicine ball work offers one of the best ways to strengthen the links between the legs (which generate power) and the arms (which deliver it). It is not uncommon for a few confused looks to cross people's faces when I start talking about the importance of the hips and legs in generating a powerful tennis stroke, but don't just take my word for it.

Look at how Nick Morgan uses his trunk and hip muscles to deliver real power to a backhand.

See, too, how Nick unleashes a forehand with a strong hip drive.

It doesn't matter if you can do one or a thousand sit-ups, if you can't use – dynamically – your side, back and trunk muscles in the correct way, then you won't be able to produce powerful shots when you need them.

That is why many of the exercises given in this section are done seated. Just try doing the exercises seated and standing – do you feel the difference? See how much more you involve your trunk when seated ... and know how much better your shots will be when you have educated those muscles to transfer the power.

It is good to work with a partner, especially when you are learning the skills involved in these exercises. They can catch the ball when you throw it and they can 'feed' it back to you to throw again (and all the throwing, catching and passing they do will do them good, too!). However, bouncing the ball off a wall is just as good and, in fact, catching and controlling a 2, 3, 4 or even 5 kg medicine ball is a vital part of medicine ball training because the act of catching and stopping recruits, trains and improves more fast-twitch muscle fibres (used in short-burst, explosive work) than just throwing: plyometrics in action! (You will find more about plyometrics below.)

Equipment

Use a rubber or plastic medicine ball – the old-fashioned leather ones won't bounce back to you. (If you can't find or afford a plastic ball then you can make a perfectly serviceable one in the same way as the DIY shot in Chapter 2 (although it will not bounce at all). If you use cable ties make sure that you file away any sharp edges.

How many throws?

Start with only two or three throws per session – as you learn the skills involved you will still get a training effect – and increase until you can manage up to 150 throws per session; any more and I have found that even Olympic throwers lose concentration, especially after a session of technical training.

Using a ball of no more than 1 kg, children can perform as many as 50 throws – as long as they build up to this number *gradually*.

Two-handed throw with steps

Start with the ball just behind your head, arms straight, hands high overhead. Take one or two steps. As you throw, when you have your left leg forwards make certain that you drive your right hip forwards, too – and vice versa.

Throw the ball against a wall, catch it over-head, step back with the rebound and throw again with the other foot in front to make a continuous sequence of throws. This exercise works the chest and anterior deltoids.

Seated side throw

This exercise strengthens the obliques (the muscles at the side of the body) and the abdominals, and is designed to enhance forehand shots from all angles.

You should start with two-handed throws, but eventually build up to one-handed and throw against a wall that is at 90 degrees to you.

One-arm kneeling throw

This throw can be adapted to improve overhead, ground and other strokes – just throw the ball from overhead, the side or from the ground: simple and effective!

This exercise may be done with a partner or the ball may be thrown against a wall: catch, control and throw again. Do an equal number of throws for each arm.

This throw strengthens the whole 'delivery chain' from the knees to the hands.

Seated or kneeling 'backhand' throw

This exercise is for the shoulders (deltoids) and the upper back (latissimus dorsi). Sit or kneel; take the ball back with both hands, one behind the ball, one beneath it, and throw it very hard at your partner or a wall. Think about backhand shots when you throw and emphasise the powerful delivery from the arm and hand that is across your body and behind the ball.

Hip drive training

This drill will teach you how to drive your hips into those power shots. Hold the ball behind you and to your side; fractionally before you begin to bring the ball overhead to throw, *drive* your hips forwards. You can make this even more effective by taking one or more steps into the throw and then making your steps faster and the throw longer (or harder if you're throwing against a wall).

This exercise is great for the trunk, legs, chest, back and arms – the whole power chain.

Speed and cardio training at home or in a hotel

Even if you are staying away from home you can carry an excellent workout in your briefcase – the skipping rope.

Type of rope

There are many different ropes out there but for theses purposes use either a leather rope or a plastic speed rope.

If you choose speed rope try and get one with bearings in the handle so that it is less likely to foul. A perfectly good speed rope can be built with a length of washing line. If you want to get sexy then a couple of bits of broom handle and two washers screwed into the ends will hold the rope and help it turn freely.

Measuring the rope

For our purposes the ideal length can be judged in the following way – hold the rope handles in your right hand and put you left foot in the rope to keep it on the floor. Pull the rope taut and if the tops of the handle come to the top of your left shoulder then it is spot on. Most ropes can be adjusted by pushing the rope through the handles and then cutting to length.

What follows are some basics that you can incorporate into your weekly workouts and are a great fall back when time or space is at a premium.

TABLE 3.2 Basic skipping moves

Bounce step
Feet togther, bounce on the balls of your feet as the rope passes under. Only one bounce per revolution.

Boxer step
As if you are running on the spot but only clear the floor by the minimum amount. Two steps per revolution (L, L, R, R, L, L, etc.).

Ski step
Feet together, bounce from side to side, as if you were doing slalom skiing.

Bell step
As per ski step, but forwards and back rather than side to side.

Split jump
On each revolution split jump right foot forwards, left foot back. Alternate each time.

Speed and cardiovascular conditioning

What we are looking for here are three elements:

1. **basic stamina** – the ability to perform for long periods at low/moderate intensity

2. **speed** – the ability to go fast for short periods

3. **speed endurance** – the ability to operate at medium/high levels repeatedly.

Aerobic conditioning

This sort of exercise promotes the ability to keep going at a moderate rate for long periods.

Aerobic means, literally, 'with oxygen'. Aerobic conditioning is sustained activity within your own 'zone', and is a vital part of every sports person's routine. You don't do much long-distance running in a tennis match, but you do use your heart and lungs, and you do need a good circulatory system to help flush away the products of fatigue and to carry oxygen and fuel to your muscles.

'But it hurts and it's boring!' I hear you cry. Well, this need not be the case at all – here are some jolly positive 'Dos':

- **do** use brisk walking, rowing, running, the step machine, cycling and even swimming to help build up your cardiovascular fitness

- **do** build up *gradually*, from as little as four minutes for your first run/ride/swim/row to an eventual minimum of 32 minutes non-stop in the zone

- **do** vary the surface you use for running – grass, sand, road, paths in the park (if safe)

- **do** get a good sweat on

- **do** finish your session with stretching exercises (in the bath or shower if you like) as this will aid recovery and increase your range of movement.

And some 'Don'ts':

- **don't** stick to just one method of aerobic training
- **don't** get exhausted
- **don't** make your arms and legs hurt
- **don't** go so fast that you can't speak
- **don't** go so hard that you're too stiff the next day.

It will be important to measure and record heart rate here to ensure that you are operating at the correct intensity. Too fast and you are defeating the object because you will be burning sugars and producing the oxidants that you should be flushing out. Too slow and you will not be working your heart hard enough.

What we are looking for is a slow jog (preferably on grass to lessen the impact on the joints) building from 16 minutes to 40 minutes over a period of weeks. (To keep variety you can swim or cycle – anything is OK as long as it is done at a consistent intensity (so five-a-side football would not be suitable).

Note that when you get the pace right you are likely to find it unnaturally slow. Don't worry: it is. Keep boredom to a minimum by splitting the run into two: eight minutes out, eight minutes back.

There is no real need to warm up as the run is at such a low impact. It is a good exercise to fit into your 'dead time' as, including a shower, you can do it in a lunch hour.

Measuring your heart rate

The heart rate you should maintain during the basic stamina phase is called your 'target heart rate'. There are several ways of arriving at this figure. Some methods for calculating the target rate take individual differences into consideration; here is one of them.

1. Subtract your age from 220 to find your *maximum heart rate*.

2. Subtract your *resting heart rate* from your *maximum heart rate* to determine your *heart rate reserve*. (Your resting heart rate can be determined by taking your pulse after sitting quietly for five minutes, before you undertake any exercise. The best time is when you are still in bed in the morning; although, if woken by an alarm, you should wait about five minutes.)

3. Take 70 per cent of your *heart rate reserve* to determine your *heart rate raise*.

4. Add your *heart rate raise* to your *resting heart rate* to find your target heart rate.

TABLE 3.3 Example of a target heart rate calculation

Maximum heart rate	220
Minus age	24
= total	196
Minus resting heart rate	60
= heart rate reserve	136
Divide by 70% or multiply by 0.7	
= heart rate raise	95
Heart rate raise + heart rate reserve	
= target rate	155

Count your pulse for 10 seconds and multiply by six to get the per-minute rate.

When checking your heart rate during a workout, take your pulse within five seconds after interrupting exercise because it starts to go down as soon you stop moving.

Speed work

An overview of the mechanics of speed and agility

| 1. | 2. | 3. |

Forward movement is achieved by the extension of the hip, knee and ankle joints: the 'drive' phase (action 1 in the accompanying illustration).

Sprinting is doing the same thing very fast, repeating it with alternate legs *more* than four times each second. Apart from a slight cross-body arm action, there should be no side-to-side movement.

As the driving foot leaves the ground, the heel of that foot should fold fast and touch the buttock, the leg coming through as a short (and therefore fast) lever (action 2).

The folded leg should be pulled through, as in action 3, to a high knee lift that will impart a 'ground reaction' and make the power of the other leg, which is now driving, more effective.

As the foot returns to the ground, it should be pulled back to make a dynamic 'active' landing.

Powerful drive and subsequent relaxation of the driving muscles will make the foot fold to the buttock, it will make the knee come through fast and high, and the pendulum effect will aid in making the active landing.

The arms should work as opposites to the legs; they should balance *and guide* the whole action – no flapping, no excessive opening and closing of the elbows (which should be kept at roughly 90 degrees) and the elbows driven back – all the best work in sprinting is done behind the body.

Forward speed is the product of stride rate and stride range. A stride range or length of two metres and a stride rate of two metres per second will give a forward velocity of eight metres per second, which equals 100 metres in 12.5 seconds – a time of which any self-respecting sports person would be proud.

Speed of muscular contraction is largely (genetically) determined by the percentage of white (fast) and red (slower) fibres found in the muscle itself. There are many other factors that influence speed: muscle fuels available, co-ordination, flexibility and muscle viscosity, gross, relative and specific strength, elastic and starting strength, correct motor programmes in the brain, motivation, an absence of wasted movement ... and many more.

This means that diet must be good; training must start with the general and become more specific (never forgetting speed – if you forget speed, you can forget winning!); good stretching and warm-up procedures *must* be followed; multi-exercise circuits *and* correct (free) weight training must be undertaken; drills must be perfect; short sprints must be undertaken regularly; sloppy practice must be ruthlessly stamped out, and good style inculcated.

However, note that acceleration, the ability to change pace, and physical and mental toughness are often more important than a high top speed.

Sprinting drills

The 'drills' described on the following pages are designed to improve both your rate and range of stride; the movements are fast and light at the start, stronger and more powerful at the end.

Introduce the drills gradually (remember ground rule 2: pace yourself). I have seen big strong men reduced to tears by the too rapid introduction of these drills: 'shin splints' can cripple a player, ruin their season and any chance of advancement (big, heavy athletes tend to suffer more than lighter ones). Once you have suffered from such injuries, they tend to recur, so be careful and take things gradually.

Remember, too, that brittle things break. Stretching is an important part of warming down. It will also help you achieve a full range of movement in the exercises you are about to perform.

The emphasis here is on quality and teaching your legs to go faster, so make sure you are well rested.

If you have ignored the call for quality until now, please register it *immediately*! These drills are the place where you teach your body to propel you fast. Just as a top-class musician will never rush through their scales, a top-class athlete has no time for sub-standard drills.

Warm-up

The same principles apply as those employed when at the gym. A fair warm-up need not take more than 20–25 minutes but will save you a world of pain in terms of injury.

An example of a warm-up routine is 10 minutes' running (two laps of a pitch/track at a jog, then stride out the lengths/straights on one more lap).

Drills

All drills must be preceded by a stretching exercise that lengthens and relates directly to the muscle or muscle group that is to be trained in the specific drill. For example, before you do the heel pick-up drill, perform a quadriceps stretch; before you do leg raises perform a straight-leg hamstring stretch (see the accompanying pictures).

Note that the drills described below will be used and referred to in the phased workouts in the next chapter of this book.

Heel pick-up

How to do it

Body upright, waist long, thigh vertical, *fast* pick-up of heels to backside (so that contact can be heard); use different rhythms throughout to avoid motor stereotypes – keep the number of lifts per leg equal (e.g. L, L, R, L, R, R, R, L, R, L, R, L, etc.)

Purpose

Conditioning of hamstrings, learning to make recovery leg a short (and therefore fast) lever

Knee pick-up

How to do it

Good posture, knees pulled fast and high to chest, keep thighs in line of running (don't splay the knees)

Purpose

Conditioning hip flexors, learning to lift knees fast and high in running action, to aid stride length and improve ground reaction

Side steps

How to do it
Good posture, side skipping, aim for height/distance on each step, keep body square to line of travel (looking back helps), stay on balls of feet

Purpose
General agility, conditioning of the adductors and abductors to avoid imbalance and injury, and provide stabilisation of prime movers

High skipping

How to do it
Good tall posture, top of head high, aim for greatest possible height and knee lift with front leg raised so that soles of shoes are visible to observers in front

Purpose
Conditioning of hip flexors and extensors, and calf muscles to teach forceful and short ground contact time

Leg raises

How to do it

Legs straight (or high kicking, chorus-girl style)

Purpose

To condition hip flexors and give dynamic stretch to hamstrings

Step and bound

How to do it

Body upright, a series of long-jump 'take-offs' with one short running step between each; aim for height and 'air time' on each take-off

Purpose

Conditioning of hip extensors, hip flexors, trunk stabilisers, calf muscles, to teach forceful drive and knee lift

Speed and agility

If you forget speed – you can forget winning!

Imagine having the ability to get into the position quickly, with plenty of time to get your racquet back, to have more time than your opponent to choose and make your shots, and to be able to recover from difficulty. All of these require speed.

Speed kills: your opponent if you've got it; you if you haven't!

The running drills described above are the basis for any athlete but specific 'compass' drills are at the very core of tennis-specific training for speed around the court.

The supernova

Take the net away and stand on the centre service line at the back of the service court. Note the 12 points where every line meets another.

How long does it take you to touch every single point with your hand, returning to the starting point after every touch?

Face where the net would be throughout – after all, that is where your opponent will be. So touch points on the right with your right hand and points on the left with your left hand. This means that you have to run sideways, backwards and forwards.

FOR ADVANCED ATHLETES ONLY

Perform the same drill wearing 1 kg ankle weights and 1 kg wrist weights. This method – performing drills with ankle and wrist weights – has brought some of the athletes I coach county, area, national and European gold medals and records. It is not a gimmick; it is a vital part of training.

Star drill

Draw an eight-pointed 'star' or compass (see picture) with each line 1 m long. Stand on the centre spot and then jump to land on each point of the compass, returning to the centre after every contact (keep facing north). You should jump immediately to and from each point – don't stop. (Foot contact time should be less than 0.5 seconds.) You must land on each point.

Practise this first of all two footed, then do it hopping – first left footed, then right footed.

FOR ADVANCED ATHLETES ONLY

When you can perform all 16 contacts, single footed, in under seven seconds, introduce a barbell of gradually increasing weight on your shoulders. I have used up to 50 kg with some athletes that I coach (mature and strong – not beginners). And remember, good posture *always*!

Speed endurance: ghosting

Here we are looking to stress the heart, lungs and body over a longer period to more intense levels. Ghosting is a conditioning routine that is commonplace in squash but rarely seen on a tennis court. Pete Nicol (arguably the leading squash player of modern times) works regularly with the Lilleshall Sports Injury and Human Performance Centre and is a firm believer in the benefits of ghosting.

The principle is very simple but very effective: replicate the demands of a tennis match on court but without a ball or an opponent.

Many squash professionals will have a video of a real match projected on to the front wall of the squash court and they play the part of one of the players making every shot in the rallies. In this way they can control the conditioning element of the workout without the limitations of a live rally.

The best way to perform this drill is with a partner and a bit of research.

Have your partner stand at the net with a stopwatch and call a succession of shots for you to 'return'. To replicate the demands of a game situation play four to eight 'points' with 30 seconds' rest between each, rest for 60 seconds and then repeat. Once you have played these two 'games' (you'll have won both of course ...) change over and have a rest while your partner works.

This drill can be as intense as you wish as your partner can work you forehand to backhand, net to baseline and so on, and the 'rallies' can be as long as you wish.

Remember: progress *slowly* and practise *quality*. The fact that there's no ball is no excuse for sloppiness!

Plyometrics

Important warning: *high-impact plyometric work can be unsafe for people with back and/or joint wear, and can place major stress on tendons in the over-21 age group or the still-growing group.*

This is a massive topic and one on which whole books are written. I have included a concise overview of the relevant bits that will get you started and add benefit and variety to your workouts.

Plyometrics is a form of conditioning that seeks to improve the muscle's ability to recruit and deploy maximum muscle action in the shortest time possible. It is therefore excellent for training speed and power within tennis.

Although plyometric exercises take different forms, the objectives can be split into two groups for our purposes:

1. **starting strength** – the ability to instantaneously recruit the maximum number of muscle fibres possible (e.g. an initial burst of speed from standing or slow pace to flat out)

2. **explosive stamina** – the ability to maintain the initial explosion of muscle contraction going over a period or distance against some resistance (e.g. repeated explosive shots during long rallies).

What follows are some basic groups of drills that will attack the upper and lower body requirements of our sport. All of the following should be done on a forgiving surface (e.g. grass or a running track), *never on tarmac*.

Knee tucks

TECHNIQUE

- Drop to a half squat and immediately explode upwards into a tuck jump.

- Land as per jump squats (see earlier).

- On touching the ground, treat it as if it were red hot and drive upwards into another tuck jump.

- Initially perform two sets of 10 tucks with two minutes' rest between sets.

- When you've got the technique nailed, build up to four sets of 20 with one minute between sets.

- Progress gradually to six sets with a one-minute rest between sets.

Multiple bounds

TECHNIQUE

- Jog in slowly, the trunk vertical, and then make flat-footed bounds.

- Maintain good posture throughout, stressing high knee action and powerful drives from the grounded leg.

- Perform three sets over 20 m with two minutes' rest.

Split jumps

TECHNIQUE

- Starting position: large stride to the front, one leg fully extended and the other at 90 degrees.

- Spring up powerfully and, changing legs, land back at the starting position. Do once on each leg for one rep.

- Perform two sets of five jumps (each side) with two minutes' rest between sets.

- Build gradually to four sets of 10 jumps (each side) with one minute's rest between sets.

Box jumps

You will need several PE benches or several sturdy, stable boxes *no more than 75 cm high.*

TECHNIQUE

- Arrange the benches or boxes at intervals of 1–2 m apart.

- Drop from one bench/box and immediately rebound, two footed on to the next and the next and the next …

- Do the same thing, but first on your left foot and then on your right.

- Do the same thing, but sideways – first one way, then the other.

Eventually you can develop your own tricks and routines.

Speed loading (resistance)

It is not uncommon for coaches and players to believe that if you run up enough steep hills then, as your legs become stronger, you will consequently move faster. Not true. If it were, then we would see rock climbers winning the 100 m gold medal at the Olympics.

Resistance work is an important part of a conditioning programme, but it should be viewed as only one of many aspects. You will get most out of this section of your work if you remember to:

use light resistance to ensure that sprinting form is not affected.

This means that near-vertical hills or 50 kg rucksacks are counter-productive. All they teach your legs to do is to run up near-vertical hills or carry 50 kg rucksacks. You need to learn to go fast! Here are a couple of ideas that will provide moderate overload while allowing you to maintain good form. There are plenty of others involving varying degrees and types of equipment. Understand the principle and then, if you like, try some ideas of your own.

DIY resistance equipment (version 1)

An ordinary car tyre (no wheel!) gives enough resistance for our purpose (and not a Mini tyre either – an old Land Rover front tyre would be best – large enough to provide good resistance and not bounce all over the place). Tie one end to a five-metre length of rope and attach the other to a weight belt or piece of seat belt (or something similar) tied around your waist. (When sprinting with this kit, make sure that the rope is taut before you set off, to avoid jarring.)

If you have a partner you can use the harness and rope to apply variable resistance.

DIY resistance equipment (version 2)

Requiring no equipment at all, incline (not hill) running is the simplest option of all, yet offers a similar degree of overload to version 1. Start with two reps of 15 m and gradually build up to a maximum of 10 reps of 20 m.

This may not seem very far but if you consider how far you would run in a game you will realise that sprinting for more than about 20 m will happen only once or twice a match and, if you go any further than that, you will probably be standing in the clubhouse!

Circuits: training on a low time budget

So far, I have thrown a number of activities at you (well over 50, in fact). How many of these you will need to employ will be examined in the next chapter, where we look at building individual training plans.

However, there is one last area of physical activity we should consider before moving on. Arguably it is the most important for any tennis player – whether they are training once a week or twice a day. It is not exactly an exercise in itself, rather a way of combining exercises to deliver an effect and, like so many brilliant and life-changing ideas, it is basically very simple.

Welcome to the wonderful world of circuit training!

- Do something fast and you will improve your speed.

- Do something many times and you will improve your stamina.

- Do it against resistance and you will get stronger.

- Do it perfectly and you will get good!

Do all the above in the same training unit and you will save time and make fantastic progress.

If I was compelled to choose one training system: weights, running, swimming, cycling or any other, I would choose properly set-up circuit training because it offers aerobic conditioning, speed, all-over strength endurance, local muscular endurance, agility, strength, determination and will power.

And here's the icing on the cake – there's no need to even leave your own home!

Setting up a circuit

In a gym, large room, garage, patio or on court, set up a series of exercises that alternate one major body part with another (legs, trunk, arms) so that while you're working your arms, your legs and trunk are recovering but your heart rate is kept high – because you don't stop working.

Circuit training is very flexible. It doesn't matter at which station you start, and you can:

- work for different load and recovery times
- perform a fixed number of repetitions at each station and see how fast you complete the whole circuit
- vary the amount of time you spend at each station
- vary the number of reps done by spending a set time at each station.

You can even vary the number of stations in a circuit by adding (or even removing) exercises.

How to do it

Begin by working your way round the circuit with a partner. Perform 20 seconds of perfect repetitions at each station. Ask your partner, who should be very strict, to check your technique. Then swap over and you check your partner's technique (while recovering at the same time). Then both move on to the next station. In this way you encourage each other and ensure that you will both get the best out of each exercise and the circuit as a whole when you come to do your circuit training for real.

When you both decide you are competent, work for 20 seconds at each station, take 10 seconds' rest while moving to the next station, then do 20 seconds on that, and so on. Keep rigidly to these load and recovery times. Eventually, you should build up to 30 seconds' work at each station with just five seconds between stations (just enough time to change over).

Sample circuit

Like any circuit, the one shown in Table 3.4 can be adapted to suit any age, gender or physical ability (for example, the press-up performed can be full or bridge, the dips can be from a bench or done in a dipping rack with a weighted belt). You will find descriptions of how to do these exercises on the pages noted.

TABLE 3.4 Circuit training

Station 1
Press ups
Perfect form! Tight stomach and back at all times and keep it all ramrod straight.

Station 2
Sit ups
Alternate sides just as before.

Station 3
Squat thrust
Fast! The same as in the mini circuits – alternate legs this time (and no sliding!)

Station 14
Abdominal sprints
Fast! Curl your chest off the floor and pump your legs as if sprinting. Try to drive your feet out horizontally – it's harder.

Station 4
Bench dips
The same as before. Perfect form – don't let your chest sag.

Station 13
Prone pull ups
Keep your middle tight and in a straight line throughout. Touch your chest on the bar for each repetition.

Station 5
Chinnies
The same as in mini-circuits.

Station 15
Shuttles
10m shuttle sprints. Flat out with nice sharp turns. Drive hard with the arms. This is where you earn the right to win that last rally! (If you are pushed for space you can always use Power skipping – sorry no excuses...)

Station 6
Split jumps
The same as in mini-circuits.

Station 12
Side jumps
Feet together side to side over the bench or breeze block. Use your arms for more lift.

Station 11
Alternate V sits
With straight arms throughout meet feet and hands in a 'jacknife'.

Station 7
Pull overs
With straight arms throughout lift the ball from above your head to directly above your chest. Return to the floor. This is one repetition.

Station 10
Two hand curl
Use the medicine ball and keep your chest up throughout. Don't let your back sag.

Station 9
Astride jumps
Use a breeze block or bench and from astride it to on top with feet together. Return to the start is one repetition.

Station 8
Crunchies
The same as in mini-circuits.

The most important rule is to focus on quality and progression. As ever, be like Milo: start small with perfect technique and progress at a rate that is sustainable (but testing) for you.

Mini-circuits

'That's all very well', I hear you cry, 'But I can't always get to the gym, so is circuit training out for me?'

Of course not! Allow me to introduce the 'mini-circuit'. (Sounds quite pleasant doesn't it?)

All you need is a doorstep the same height as a PE bench (better still, see if you can get your tennis club to invest in a PE bench) and a mat. Simple, yet the results can be amazing.

How to do it

There are three exercises in mini-circuit 1, four in mini-circuit 2 and five in mini-circuit 3 with 20 repetitions (to a count of 20) for every exercise in each circuit. There is no pause or rest between the exercises in any of the circuits. (You may rest between circuits.)

As ever, *make each repetition perfect*. Never sacrifice quality for speed of execution or number of repetitions.

Make certain you can do the required 20 repetitions of all the given exercises properly before you start – that might mean a week or two of 'training to train', but don't worry: every time you practise (and if you practise for perfection) you'll be improving your fitness and, therefore, your game.

Time how long it takes you to perform each circuit, record the time, and take at least six minutes' rest before you do the next circuit.

Mini-circuit 1 (see Table 3.5) is designed to work the chest muscles, arms, back and abdominals, and to boost your general fitness and ability to cope with intense rallies. The best time I've ever seen for this circuit is 48.5 seconds, by Isobelle Donaldson, Scottish international heptathlete and RAF champion.

TABLE 3.5 Mini-circuit 1

Squat thrusts Start in the front support position, hands on the bench or doorstep. Pull both knees up until they are just above the front of the bench and drive back to full extension as vigorously as you can. Do 20 reps. Keep your back flat.		
Burpees With hands on the bench, do a two-footed jump up on to the bench; drop back to the floor immediately, driving your legs back into the front support position, keeping hands on the bench. Do 20 reps. Keep your head up and your back flat throughout.	 	
Press-ups Perform a press-up with your hands on the bench. Do 20 reps.		

Mini-circuit 2 (see Table 3.6) is designed to work your trunk – the abdominals, obliques (sides) and back. In this circuit, more effort must be devoted to the perfect execution of the exercises than to the time taken.

TABLE 3.6 Mini-circuit 2

Oblique sit-ups For the abdominals. Bend your knees so that both feet are flat on floor. Keep feet and knees together. Fingertips touching ears. Sit up so that your feet remain in contact with the floor and your left elbow touches your right knee. Don't go any further forwards than this. *Do not ram or jerk your head between your knees* – you will hurt your back if you do! Lie back so that both elbows lightly touch the ground. Do 20 reps.		
Leg raise left and right (page 82) For the side muscles (obliques). Keep your backside tucked in and your body, from head to toe, ramrod straight. Your legs should be straight and your feet and knees together. Do 20 reps.		
Superman (page 83) For your back. Keep your head up and your back flat in a strong bridge. Do 20 reps.		
Chinnies (page 84) For your abdominals. Do 20 reps.		

Mini-circuit 3 (see Table 3.7) is designed to boost general fitness, agility, and your ability to cope with and recover from severe rallies. It will also work to strengthen your legs, which generate as much as 80 per cent of the power of your shots and get you into position in time to play those shots accurately.

With all the exercises in this circuit, keep your body upright, your chest high, your head up, your backside and your stomach in, and your back flat. Maintain good posture at all times.

TABLE 3.7 Mini-circuit 3

Heel pick-up (page 101) Heel to just *touch* back-side, keep thighs vertical. Do 20 reps. See the difference between the incorrect position (photo 1), and the correct position (photo 2).		
Knee pick-up (page 101) Running on the spot, raise your thighs at least parallel to the floor.		
Bouncing foot twists Keeping your feet together, bounce through 90 degrees – from '10 to' to '10 past' the hour. Do 20 reps.		

TABLE 3.7 Mini-circuit 3 – continued

Split jumps
(page 108) Double shoulder width
between feet. Do 20 reps.

Tuck jumps
Keeping your trunk vertical, jump
with both feet together, tucking in
both knees so that your thighs are
parallel to the ground. Do 20 reps.

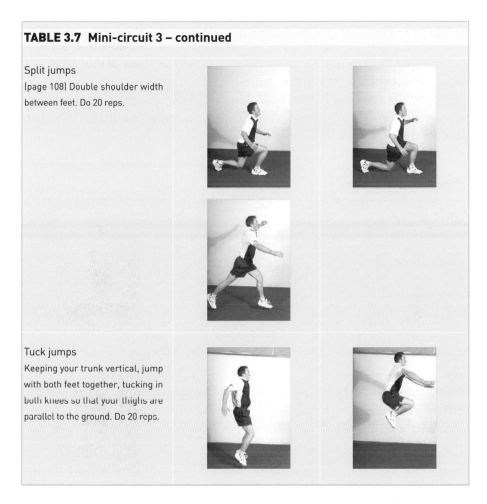

Now you have all the tools you will need, turn to Chapter 4 to find out how best to put them to good use.

4 PUTTING IT ALL TOGETHER

aim:

- To provide you with sample training structures in which you will utilise all the elements and tools described in the previous chapters.

The nature of your training will depend on a number of factors:

- how much time you have at your disposal (or have committed to training)
- your objectives
- whether or not it is the tennis season
- whether you fall in to one of the 'special' groups detailed in the Introduction.

It is important that you tailor your own programme. Think about what you need for your game. Whatever the conditioning routine you undertake, you should constantly refer back to how it will fit the specific objectives you have set yourself for improvement.

Whatever the type, intensity or frequency of your training, always remember our three ground rules:

1. be honest
2. pace yourself
3. quality before quantity – *always*.

Building a training plan

There are many books on the market that offer up set à la carte training schedules. However, as no two athletes have the same strengths and weaknesses, are built in the same way or are even the same age, beware of such one-size-fits-all approaches.

If you have followed this book so far, you will already have an understanding of your particular starting point and any areas of weakness that will need to be addressed in your training schedule. In addition, you should have considered how much time is available for off-court training, where that is in your week and how much you are willing to commit.

This information, coupled with that provided in this section can assist you in building a highly individualised training plan that will help you to achieve your tennis goals.

In this chapter, we will consider how to develop the 'Three Ss':

- **strength** – more, accurately power – the ability to deliver strength *fast*

- **speed** – to enable you to get there first

- **stamina** – how to keep going for longer.

The main principles

Look at the word 'fit'. We all know what it means, but it can also be a guide to how you can get a little extra from your training and what that extra should, or could, be:

- **frequency** – how often you train

- **intensity** – how hard you train

- **time** – how long you spend in training.

How much extra you are willing to do depends on your reason for playing in the first place. You might be a social player or a title contender – there are no judgements made on the relative merits, each reason is as important as any other. All I am looking to do is to help you succeed, and the definition of success is different for different people.

For each of the sample scenarios presented below, consider the ideas presented in the following diagram.

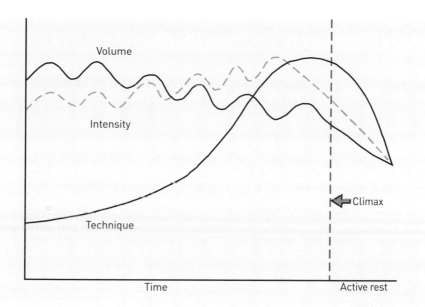

The 'time' line in the diagram depends on your need: it could be a whole year for the top-class competitor who uses early matches as practice; it could be two months for the less ambitious.

The 'intensity' line means that you reduce quantity but increase quality.

Important notes

- First, you will need to do plenty of general fitness and strength work – work hard, then recover, work hard, then recover – hence the wave-like progression of the 'volume' line.

- Gradually replace quantity with quality, making your training more intense – note the broken line. As John McEnroe says, too many people lack intensity of attitude (and that includes training).

- A similar diagram, made out for a child, will have little in the way of gradients because peaking is often too stressful for many children and their progress should be smooth and gradual.

- Reduce both volume and intensity as you get closer to the big match of the season (you won't play well if you're exhausted).

- Smoothly *increase* the amount of technique training as you approach 'the big one' (but always do some fast and technical work, wherever you are in the season).

- 'Active rest' is just that: reduced intensity, volume and technical work – but never stopping altogether.

- If you play social tennis all year round – great!

- If you wish to give yourself a specific goal, then select a league or club match that is more important to you than the others and plan accordingly – you'll surprise everyone and win easily!

Sample scenarios

Scenario 1

Player
Ten years old, male or female, parents very keen for success, takes tennis lessons twice weekly.

Ensure adequate time for homework, sleep, company of friends and family, free-choice activities, *other sports*, out-of-school activities like music, reading, even computer games, and he/she must have time to play as a child, with other children.

Frequency
2 x formal tennis lessons or matches; 1 x a session that can include two or three of the activities listed in the training chapters, including something different every session, *with an emphasis on performance, not results*!

Intensity
Good attitudes and enthusiasm must be inculcated, of course, and the properly motivated and informed child will try very hard to do well, but must be restrained sometimes from doing too much.

Time
Just like our potential champion in Scenario 4 – whatever it takes. But do not let any one thing rob a child of his/her childhood.

Example training diary

MONDAY
    Conditioning session
 	
    Mini-circuits – PB in MC1

TUESDAY   Won at conkers at break-time – I've now got a 12-er!

WEDNESDAY
    Coaching session (60 mins)
 	
    Concentrated on volleying and half-court work

THURSDAY   Five-a-side (45 mins); great fun – played in goal for one quarter (definitely not my forte) – scored two
FRIDAY   –
SATURDAY   Match (or coaching) (90 mins)
SUNDAY   –

Scenario 2

Player

Fifty years old, female, plays once a week to 'keep fit'.

Look back at the Martini gym section in Chapter 3 and adapt it to the facilities you have at home. Make some of the equipment described and use it – or go to the club – *one* more time each week, and do a modified circuit: warm up with a gradually increasing amount of skipping then do your circuit followed by a few minutes' light stretching.

Set up your circuit with as many stations as possible (at least 15) and do six perfect repetitions of each exercise in a smooth and rhythmic manner. Take 15 seconds between each exercise and do the circuit once only (for now). Next week, do seven repetitions, and the following week do eight ... and so on. Make your cool-down smooth: use non-ballistic stretching or even yoga. Keep a diary of your training and always give yourself at least one day of rest before you play your weekly game.

Be strong minded! Your family should be supportive – you could even get them to join in. Take pride in your increasing fitness and improved looks.

Osteoporosis, heart disease and the thousand-and-one natural shocks the flesh is heir to are no fun, and tennis and circuit training offer the best possible way to avoid all of them. It's simple – use it or lose it! The older you get the more accurate this truism.

Frequency

2 x per week: 1 game, 1 circuit.

Intensity

Circuit: easy to begin with. Game: moderate.

Time

Circuit (1st session): skipping, stretching and circuit – 30 minutes inclusive. Game: 1 hour. Total: 90 minutes each week.

Remember: if you are starting from scratch give yourself a chance – you will have to 'train to train'. Start with low intensity and low repetitions, and build your capacity steadily.

Example training diary

MONDAY 　Rest	
TUESDAY 　Circuit training	
WEDNESDAY 　Rest	
THURSDAY 　Circuit training	
FRIDAY 　Rest	
SATURDAY 　'Winter Woolies' league doubles match (6–2, 6–4)	
SUNDAY 　Club day. American tournament (2 hours of intermittent doubles)	

Scenario 3

Player

Eighteen years old, female, winning county titles.

This is a 'common-sense training guide' so let's consider: are you in the sixth form, your first year at university or your first job? Whatever, this is a hard time for you and you'll need to devote time to your social life, study of one sort or another, relaxation and recovery. You'll also need to be strong minded because of peer pressure to go drinking, clubbing and late-nighting. Better to associate with like-minded, more dedicated, sports people if possible ...

One day: play a game – for real; try to win but remember to experiment with new techniques as you get faster and stronger.

One day: do a real circuit session (this should be the hardest day of your training week).

One day: you can do another, shorter, session on court, the running drills and compass drills, and do a medicine ball or weights session immediately afterwards.

One day: do an aerobic run, ride, swim or row, followed by mini-circuits.

Remember: if you miss out one of the training components you can include it next week, but log everything in a training diary so that you can make sure you do all the components in your two-week training 'cycle'.

The closer you are to a match, or the tennis season, the more specific your training must be – it is not a good idea to go for a 45-minute hard swim the night before the most important match of the season, for instance.

Frequency

4 x per week.

Intensity

2 x hard, 2 x moderate.

Time

Game: 90 mins. Circuit: 1 hour. Drills, skills and medicine ball: 1 hour. Run, ride, swim or row and mini-circuits: 1 hour Total: four and a half hours each week.

Example training diary

(This is intended as an illustration only – not as a prescription for any individual.)

MONDAY
Rest

TUESDAY
Hard session
Circuit training (see below) with coach to spot and shout!
Very hard – ow!

WEDNESDAY
60-min hit with training partner and coach

THURSDAY
Sprint drills with partner (25 mins)
Medicine ball session with partner (35 mins)

FRIDAY
Rest

SATURDAY
Game (or coaching)

SUNDAY
Recovery bike ride
(40 mins steady state)

| **MONDAY** |
| Hard session (lifts and mini circuits) |
| One-hand snatch 1 x 5 @ 20 kg, 2 x 4 @ 25 kg, 3 x 3 @ 30 kg |
| Clean and jerk 1 x 5 @ 45 kg, 2 x 4 @ 50 kg, 3 x 3 @ 52.5 kg |
| Mini-circuits MC1 = 69 secs, MC2 = 82 secs, MC3 = 79 secs |

| **TUESDAY** |
| Rest |

| **WEDNESDAY** |
| 60-min hit with training partner and coach |

| **THURSDAY** |
| Sprint drills with partner (25 mins) |
| Medicine ball session with partner (35 mins) |

| **FRIDAY** |
| Rest |

| **SATURDAY** |
| Game (or coaching) |

| **SUNDAY** |
| Recovery run (40 mins steady state) |
| Mini-circuits MC1 = 68 secs, MC2 = 84 secs, MC3 = 72 secs |

Scenario 4

Player

Twenty-two years old, male, aiming to win national titles.

Commitment and determination are required. Remember what Napoleon said was the secret of success:

> *Ceaseless activity, concentration of forces and keeping the ideal, the goal and the ambition always burning clear in the mind.*

All components of the regime: weights, medicine ball, practice matches, skill practice, skipping, drills, aerobic conditioning, stretching, circuits and mini-circuits must be done throughout the week. The aerobic conditioning should be easy, not a grinding slog (it would drill in the wrong type of movement anyway). Ensure correct diet, adequate sleep and recovery, or adaptation will not take place and you'll get no benefit from your training.

Frequency

6/7 days each week.

Intensity

3 x hard, 2 x moderate, 1 x easy, 1 x free choice (which may well be rest).

Time

Whatever it takes!

A schedule of this intensity is definitely not the place for anyone to start. This is intended as an example snapshot only, and might represent just one week in a 12-week build-up to the season or a key event.

Example training diary

WEEK ONE

MONDAY
Hard day
One-hand snatch 2 x 4 @ 30 kg, 2 x 4 @ 35 kg, 2 x 2 @ 37.5 kg, 3 x 1 @ 42.5 kg
Clean and jerk 1 x 4 @ 50 kg, 2 x 4 @ 60 kg, 2 x 2 @ 65 kg, 4 x 1 @ 70 kg
Front squats 3 x 6 @ 70 kg
15 mins skipping

TUESDAY
Moderate day

Sprint drills (30 mins) followed by 45 mins ball machine

Mini-circuits MC1 = 69 secs, MC2 = 82 secs, MC3 = 79 secs

WEDNESDAY
Hard day

45 mins coaching on court plus circuits

THURSDAY
Moderate day

90 mins hitting with partner

Medicine ball drills with partner

FRIDAY
Rest

SATURDAY
Hard day
Match practice – 120 mins
Medicine ball drills
Star squats 3 x 8 @ 50 kg

SUNDAY
Easy day

Swim – 1 mile, steady pace

5 DIET AND NUTRITION

aim:

* To help you understand the key elements of nutrition and how very small changes can have a very significant impact on your preparation

Diet as refuelling

At levels outside the top flight, diet comes lower down the list of things that can have a dramatic impact on performance – but if you wish to develop the outlook you have on your preparation for your sport you may want to include some sensible and moderate changes to your diet.

The reason that this topic has been left until last is not because it is of least importance. It is just that it is our experience that diet is one of the hardest things to change, as it is likely to be one of your longest-standing habits. However, if you have taken the structured approach to your body conditioning that the previous chapters have suggested then you may find yourself more open to making changes to your diet. Many athletes see diet as offering a way to enhance all their existing good work; they recognise its ability to add to, as well as detract from, all their hard work.

Although I am not suggesting you become a monk, real results can be gained by making just slight adjustments to your eating patterns. Again, it comes down to the individual: if it's important to you, you may want to make some changes, and if other things take precedence in your life then you may not. It's OK either way – just be *honest* with yourself.

At the risk of repeating myself – the most important thing, as you will have seen throughout this book, is to be honest with yourself. If you are not, then all you are doing is setting yourself up to fail ... and you will feel guilty when you do.

By the end of this chapter you should have a general understanding of how what you put into your mouth affects your performance. The good news is that it's not rocket science. There are just some very basic rules to observe.

Special considerations for pre-adolescent and adolescent children

Children require more energy than do adolescents or adults during sports that include walking and running. The energy cost of any given activity, when calculated per kg of body mass, is considerably higher in children and adolescents than in adults. Also, the younger the child, the higher the relative cost. A seven-year-old child, for example, would require as much as 25–30 per cent more energy per kg body mass than an adult for the same activity at the same intensity, while a 14-year-old may require up to 15 per cent more.

The reason for this relative 'wastefulness' of energy in children is the lack of adequate co-ordination between their muscle groups. Consequently, it is likely that the energy cost will decrease as their proficiency and co-ordination increase.

The basic food groups and what they do

Carbohydrate

Carbohydrate consumed before, during and after exercise can enhance performance.

This is the most important nutrient for your working muscles and should make up 60–70 per cent of the energy in your diet. When eaten, carbohydrate is broken down into glucose and is then absorbed into the blood from where it is either used as a fuel or stored as glycogen. Storage capacity, however, is limited, so a frequent supply of glucose is needed to maintain levels. Low stores will result in poor performance and an increased risk of injury.

Your requirement for carbohydrate can be calculated using the following equation:

weight (kg) x level of training = carbohydrate requirement per day

'Level of training' is classified as follows:

- light (less than one hour per day) – 4–5
- moderate (one to two hours per day) – 6–7
- heavy (more than three hours per day) – 8–10.

Therefore, the range for a 75 kg person undergoing moderate training would be 450–525 g of carbohydrate per day. The table on page 171 of the Appendix contains a list of foods and the portion sizes needed to provide 50 g of carbohydrate.

How to increase carbohydrate intake

Carbohydrate intake can be boosted by eating more:

- bread – eat plenty and, if it is fresh, cut it thicker
- rice – or other grains such as oatmeal, bulgar wheat and couscous
- fruit – as part of a meal, as a snack or added to dishes
- pasta – or noodles
- cereals – can be eaten at any time of day
- veg – fresh, frozen or canned (e.g. baked beans, chickpeas, kidney beans).

Other ideas to increase carbohydrate intake include:

- snacking on high-carbohydrate foods
- eating sugary foods that are energy-dense
- using high-carbohydrate drinks (e.g. fruit juice, soft drinks, low-fat milkshakes, sports drinks).

Fat

Fat is a concentrated form of energy. It provides twice the number of calories as the same weight of protein or carbohydrate. All fat, whether butter, margarine, olive oil or the fat on your kebab meat, has the same number of calories for a given weight, and too much fat in your diet, especially too much saturated fat, can lead to health problems such as heart disease. High-fat diets also contain high levels of cholesterol, which is problematic in high quantities. Fat is, however, essential in the diet because it acts as a carrier for the fat-soluble vitamins (A, D, E and K). It should not, though, make up any more than 20 per cent of your energy intake. Unlike carbohydrate, which can only be stored in limited amounts, there is always sufficient fat available as fuel for exercise and even the leanest of competitors has a large reserve of fat for energy.

Here are some simple methods that can help you to reduce the fat content of your diet.

- Cut out margarine and butter, which are virtually all fat, and replace them with jam or honey, which contain virtually no fat.

- Eat low-fat dairy products (cheese and yoghurts) instead of full-fat products.

- Grill, poach, bake, steam, microwave or casserole food instead of frying it.

- If frying food, use an oil-substitute spray instead of adding fat.

- Choose lean cuts of meat, cut off any visible fat and skim off visible fat when cooking.

- Remove the skin from poultry.

- Keep your intake of pastry products to a minimum.

- If you eat chips, choose thick-cut over French fries, and oven chips over fried chips.

- Fill jacket potatoes with moist fillings such as beans instead of butter, margarine and cheese.

- Make custards and sauces with low-fat milk.

- Choose reduced-fat versions of muffins, cakes, puddings, and so on.

If you are serious about reducing your fat intake you should also learn to read food labels because '95 per cent fat free' does not necessarily mean that only 5 per cent of the calories come from fat! Companies want to sell products and what better way to do so than to say they are good for you? However, there are easy ways to see through these claims.

First, read the ingredient list on the label. Ingredients are listed in descending order. If fat is in the top three or listed several times by various names, then the food is probably high in fat. Fats may be hidden under the following aliases: vegetable fat, vegetable oil, animal fat, shortening, lard, cream, butter or margarine.

Second, if you are very serious, look for the fat content by weight of the food and work out the percentage of fat in the food. Nutritional information is listed on the packaging. A food label may say that there is 10 g of fat in 100 g of a product – *great*, less than 20 per cent fat! Or is it? Remember that fat contains 9 kcal per gram as opposed to the 4 kcal per gram in carbohydrate and protein. Therefore, to work out the true percentage of fat in a food you need to multiply the number of grams of fat per 100 g by nine and then find out what percentage this represents of the number of calories per 100 g. Confused? Try the following example.

Whole milk
The label says:
- 4 g fat per 100 ml
- 69 kcal per 100 ml

The calculations are as follows:

4 g x 9 kcal = 36 kcal from fat in 100 ml
36 kcal/69 kcal = 52 per cent fat of calories come from fat.

So, although whole milk is quite low in fat compared to many foods, in fact *52 per cent of the calories it provides are derived from fat!*

The moral of this story is: do not believe everything you read on the packet.

Special considerations for pre-adolescent and adolescent children

Compared with adults, children and adolescents use more fat and less carbohydrate during prolonged exercise. This is probably due to the fact that children tend to rely more on aerobic energy metabolism (in which fat is the major energy source) than on anaerobic metabolism (in which muscle glycogen is the major energy source). Whether this preferential use of fat as an energy source has any implications for nutritional recommendations has yet to be determined. However, it is clear that there is no evidence to suggest that children should consume more than 30 per cent of their total energy intake as fat.

Protein

Protein is used to replace cells and build new tissue. That's why it's essential for maintaining and building muscle mass. However, there is no evidence that a high protein intake enhances metabolic efficiency or increases muscle bulk so high-protein diets are simply a waste of money! Current evidence does suggest, however, that protein requirements are increased as a result of strength, speed and endurance training, so an active person will need more than a sedentary Joe. Remember, though, that any protein consumed in excess of requirements is converted by the body into energy or, more likely, stored by the body as fat.

The amount of protein in an adult's diet should be in the range of 1.2–1.7 g/kg per day. Therefore, for a 75 kg player, the amount of protein in the diet should be between 90 and 128 g per day.

Including a variety of protein-rich foods in your diet will increase your protein intake. However, a lot of these foods may also be high in fat, so make wise choices. The table on page 172 of the Appendix contains a list of foods and the portion sizes needed to provide 10 g of protein.

Special considerations for pre-adolescent and adolescent children

To facilitate growth and development, the daily protein requirements per unit body weight are higher for children than for adults. For highly active children and adolescents, needs may reach 2 g per kg weight per day.

Vitamins and minerals

Vitamins and minerals are essential in your diet, but do you need to become a walking pillbox to get enough? The simple answer is no. If you are eating a well-balanced diet that includes foods from all of the main food groups (fruit and veg, breads and cereals, dairy products, meat and fish or alternatives) you are unlikely to be deficient in vitamins or minerals. Taking vitamin and mineral supplements is not necessary if you do not have any proven deficiencies. If, however, you do decide to take a supplement, please heed the following advice.

- Check with your chemist that you have chosen a suitable supplement.

- Check that it will not interfere with any other supplements or medication that you take.

- Follow the manufacturer's dosage instructions – do not double the dose for luck!
- Remember that 'mega' doses of vitamins or minerals, or taking large doses of single vitamins or minerals, can be harmful to your health and will not improve performance.

Eating to lose weight (fat)

The secret to losing fat mass is calories: if you're eating too many and/or not 'burning' enough off, it is impossible to lose fat.

To lose fat you need to create an energy deficit either through decreasing your energy intake or increasing your energy expenditure; a combination of the two is best. However, if you are already pretty active it may be difficult to further increase your energy expenditure, so decreasing your energy intake may be the best path for you. The reduction in your energy intake should not be so large as to affect your health or performance; most people need to subtract 500–800 calories from their energy intake in order to lose weight.

Losing fat, not muscle

The goal is to lose fat, not lean body mass (muscle). Ideally, your body fat should be monitored throughout the period of weight loss. If fat mass loss does not equate with weight loss then it is possible that you are losing lean body mass, which is not good for performance. This may happen if energy restrictions are too high and weight loss occurs too rapidly. If you find you are losing lean body mass you may need to adjust your dietary plan.

Rate of loss

Safe and effective weight loss should not exceed 2 lb (about 1 kg) per week. If you are losing more than this, it is again likely that you are losing lean body mass (see above). Initially, the rate of weight loss will be high and may represent more than 1 kg a week. However, as time passes the rate will gradually decrease and may represent half a pound per week or less after several months.

Energy intake breakdown

Your weight loss diet should be made up of approximately 60–70 per cent carbohydrate, 10–20 per cent protein and less than 20 per cent fat. The recommended carbohydrate intake is similar to that for optimal training and so should not hinder your performance; remember that a high carbohydrate intake is needed for hard training. Carbohydrate is also protein-sparing (it prevents muscles being broken down for energy) and, contrary to popular opinion, it is not fattening. Low-carbohydrate diets will only lead to lowered carbohydrate stores, poor performance and muscle breakdown.

If some 10–20 per cent of your intake comes from protein, this will provide your body with sufficient protein to maintain muscle mass without you being at risk of consuming an excess that will be stored as fat. Fat intake should make up less than 20 per cent of your total calories; excess fat will also be stored as body fat. However, it is not necessary to drop below 10 per cent fat, and cutting all fat from your diet can actually slow muscle growth, decrease strength and decrease energy levels. A low-fat diet is much better for weight loss than a non-fat diet.

You should try to combine carbohydrate and protein at each meal. Eating carbohydrate by itself causes a rapid rise in blood sugar and insulin. This promotes fat storage and causes 'rebound hypoglycaemia' (low blood sugar), leading to hunger pangs – not good if you're trying to lose weight! By combining foods properly, you can control your blood sugar and insulin, keep your energy levels steady and enhance muscle gain, while minimising fat storage.

Quality versus quantity

Fat-loss programmes are not 'starvation diets' or excuses to eat a small amount of crap! Losing fat mass without losing muscle mass is possible, but only if you consume a sensible amount of quality calories. Your diet should include foods from every food group: grains/cereals, veg, fruit, dairy products, meat and fish. Good sources of carbohydrate include rice, potatoes, beans, pasta, breakfast cereals and bread. Good sources of protein include low-fat dairy products, chicken, turkey, fish and lean red meat.

Eating and competition

Before matches/training

After a good kip, your carbohydrate stores will be almost drained and you will be fairly dehydrated, unless you are prone to indulging in midnight feasts! You need to account for these factors before training and matches.

A high-carbohydrate meal – which is also low in fat, fibre and bulk – three hours before matches and training, is recommended. This will enhance performance by increasing the amount of carbohydrate available late in the exercise session (i.e. towards the end of the half when you are flagging). However, if you cannot eat three hours before exercise, due to early-morning training or nerves, remember that something is better than nothing. Try to eat a high-carbohydrate snack such as a bowl of cereal, some toast and jam, a cereal bar or some fruit. Alternatively, have a carbohydrate drink instead of anything solid.

It is important that you also ensure you are fully hydrated prior to exercise. Beginning exercise in a dehydrated state will impair your performance. As a general rule you should try to consume a pint of fluid (not alcohol!) before going to bed and a pint on waking. You should then top this up at a rate of one pint per hour up until one hour pre-exercise. Finally, 20 minutes before you start playing or training you should try to consume another half pint.

During matches/training

Prolonged exercise challenges our carbohydrate stores and our ability to regulate body temperature. Ingesting a carbohydrate–electrolyte drink, of appropriate concentration, during training and competing will help to address these limiting factors.

Ingesting carbohydrate during exercise increases blood glucose availability and uptake by the working muscles. This increases the use of glucose as an energy source, as opposed to muscle glycogen (stored carbohydrate), and creates a 'glycogen-sparing' effect. This results in more carbohydrate being available later on in the match or session, and maintains your ability to use carbohydrate as a fuel. This helps prevent physical and mental fatigue.

Some 30–60 g of carbohydrate, or 600–1200 ml of isotonic carbohydrate-electrolyte drink per hour of exercise is recommended. This is a fairly large volume of fluid, so it is best to drink it in smaller volumes (150–300 ml) at regular intervals (every 15–20 minutes). If carbohydrate drinks are not available, drink the same volume of water, diluted fruit juice or squash.

Post-match/training

Following prolonged activity, your carbohydrate stores will need refilling and you will need to replace any fluids you have lost. Performance is only reproducible if you do so. You should start to replace the energy used immediately after the match/session. Waiting, even for 30 minutes, wastes valuable time that could be being used to ensure that your next training session or match is not below par.

The following guidelines are useful for post-exercise energy intake.

- Consume 50 g carbohydrate *as soon as possible* in liquid form (1 litre 6 per cent isotonic drink) or as easily digestible carbohydrate (dried fruit, sugar-based sweets).

- Your first meal after exercise should be high in carbohydrate and low in fat.

- Aim to consume 10 g carbohydrate per kg body weight in the first 24 hours of recovery.

- If it is not possible to consume this amount as solid carbohydrate, top it up with carbohydrate drinks.

Rehydration is as important as consuming enough carbohydrate. To achieve full rehydration, you will need to consume 150–200 per cent of the fluid lost during exercise. For example, someone losing 2 kg of body mass during exercise will need to consume three to four litres of fluid to rehydrate themselves completely. Drinking plain water is not as beneficial as drinking fluid with added sodium as this will prevent increased urine production, stimulate thirst and improve absorption. Isotonic carbohydrate drinks are ideal for use after exercise. However, do not consume drinks that contain caffeine (i.e. Coke). Caffeine is a diuretic and will cause further water loss through urination, and therefore further dehydration.

To sum up ...
Before matches/training

- Consume 600 ml (one pint) fluid before you go to bed and 600 ml when you get up.

- Consume a high-carbohydrate meal three hours before exercise.

- Consume 600 ml of fluid per hour prior to exercise.
- Consume 250–500 ml of fluid 20 minutes before exercise.

During matches/training

- Consume 30–60 g carbohydrate per hour.

Recovery from matches/training

- Consume 50 g carbohydrate as soon as possible post-exercise; continue this intake hourly up until the first solid meal.
- The first meal should contain 1–1.5 g/kg carbohydrate.
- Consume 10 g/kg carbohydrate in the first 24 hours of recovery.
- Consume 150–200 per cent of fluid lost in order to rehydrate fully.

Fluids

Fluids are possibly the most important and most commonly overlooked dietary component. Water is very important to the effective operation of your body, and even small reductions in body water (dehydration) will dramatically and quickly affect performance and, in severe cases, endanger life.

Fluid is needed to:

- avoid dehydration and the reduction in performance associated with it
- regulate body temperature
- maintain the function of virtually all the cells in the human body
- lubricate joints and eyes
- get rid of waste products from the body.

It is essential that you consume adequate fluid on a daily basis – not just when you are training or playing, although you will need to increase the amount you take in at these times. A good daily intake is important as it teaches your body to tolerate and absorb larger amounts of fluid, which means that you will not feel uncomfortably bloated during training and matches. As for training to 'tolerate dehydration' – you can't. This is like saying that a car can learn to tolerate an empty radiator – it is absolute codswallop!

Another commonly held myth, as we have already seen, is that 'sweating will help you lose weight' – rubbish, again! People who train in waterproofs (or even bin bags) in an attempt to lose weight may as well kiss goodbye to optimal performance. Although this practice probably results in instant weight loss, the weight will be replaced as soon as rehydration takes place. However, if those who try this regime fail to rehydrate so as to maintain their weight loss, they will find themselves having to cope with the effects of dehydration, which will be a lot more harmful to them and their performance than a little extra weight could ever be.

The effects of dehydration

During all types of activity, heat is produced and lost from the body via sweat. Hard exercise may require up to one litre per hour of fluid intake; however, few players will meet these demands. This is especially worrying when you consider that performance can be significantly impaired by as little as 2 per cent dehydration, and the greater the loss of body water the more pronounced the reduction in performance (a loss of 5 per cent of body mass can decrease performance by 30 per cent).

Recent studies have shown that there is no critical point of dehydration at which performance becomes impaired. Instead, there is a gradual erosion of performance as the degree of dehydration increases. Heart rate rises, you feel that you are working harder and body temperature regulation becomes more difficult with every percentage of water loss. But the effects creep up on you, so you may not even notice it happening until it's too late!

How much fluid do you need?

The amount lost through breathing, sweating and excretion varies from person to person and depends on age, climate, diet and the amount of exercise you do. However, the average man should consume at least 2.9 litres (6 pints) of water per day and the average women at least 2 litres (4.5 pints) per day. Some of this will be in the food you eat, so aiming for 1.5–2 litres of liquid per day should be adequate for the average, sedentary person. You will then need extra fluid to cover any activity you do, such as training and playing.

Special considerations for pre-adolescent and adolescent children

Special attention must be paid to prevent dehydration in children, especially in hot/humid climates.

Because of the higher energy cost for them of performing physical activities, children produce more metabolic heat and therefore need to dissipate relatively more heat than adults. As the evaporation of sweat is the main avenue for heat dissipation, this may result in excessive losses of body fluid and electrolytes such as salt. Importantly, in children core body temperature increases faster than in adults – so it is essential to prevent dehydration in children. The main strategy to use should be to enhance thirst and educate the athlete, their parents and coaches: they need to drink frequently even when they are not thirsty. To encourage drinking and enhance thirst, the beverage in question should be tasty, and include glucose and small amounts of salt.

Weight as an indicator of fluid loss

Using weight as an indicator of fluid loss is very useful. By weighing yourself immediately before and after training/matches you can estimate how much fluid you have lost (as you lose fluid from your body you lose weight).

- One kilo of weight loss equals one litre (1.75 pints) of fluid loss – this needs to be replaced *as soon as possible* after exercise.

- If you have lost fluid, consuming the same amount as was lost will not rehydrate you; you will need to consume 150–200 per cent of the amount lost in order to fully account for it. This is because over the next few hours you will still be losing fluid by continuing to sweat and through urinating, so simply drinking the amount that was lost will not do.

- Try to standardise weighing conditions; your scales should be on the same level surface each time you weigh yourself to ensure that you get accurate and consistent readings.

- Weigh yourself in minimal clothing, and towel off beforehand – being wet will artificially increase your weight, especially if you are wearing sweat- or water-soaked clothes.

When to drink

It is not just a case of drinking when you become thirsty as thirst is a poor indicator of fluid needs. Indeed, if you wait until you are thirsty, this will probably mean that you are already dehydrated and your performance will be affected despite any intake of fluid.

Ideally, during training and matches, you should drink every 15–20 minutes to remain fully hydrated (i.e. to make sure you have enough water in your body).

Water, however, may not be the ideal solution for fluid replacement during exercise; isotonic carbohydrate drinks are better. They not only help you to avoid dehydration, but also to maintain the availability of carbohydrate, which is the body's fuel.

TABLE 5.1 Symptoms of dehydration (as a percentage of body weight loss)

% body weight loss	Symptoms
0.5	Thirst
2	Stronger thirst, discomfort, appetite loss
3	Dry mouth, and reduced, darkened urine
4	Increased effort, flushed skin, impatience, apathy
5	Difficulty concentrating
6	Impaired temperature regulation
8	Dizziness, laboured breathing, confusion
10	Spasticity, imbalance, swollen tongue delirium
11	Kidney failure, circulatory insufficiency

DIY sports drinks

Well-formulated sports drinks contain the correct amounts of carbohydrate and electrolytes (sodium and potassium; don't worry about the chemistry just trust us – they are important) to maximise the absorption of the drink and provide the body with sufficient fluid and carbohydrate to optimise performance.

Commercially available drinks are fine but can be expensive. You can make your own using the following recipes. It is difficult to recreate commercial sports drinks accurately so it is essential you measure the ingredients you are using carefully so that the composition of the drink is correct.

Different drinks are suitable for different conditions, as described below.

For normal training and playing conditions

These are called 'isotonic drinks' and are 6–7 per cent carbohydrate.

- 50–70 g sugar
- 1 litre warm water
- 1–1.5 g salt
- sugar-free squash for flavour

or

- 200 ml ordinary fruit squash
- 800 ml water
- 1–1.5 g salt

or

- 500 ml unsweetened fruit juice
- 500 ml water
- 1–1.5 g salt

When playing or training conditions are hotter than normal

These are called 'hypotonic drinks' and are 2–3 per cent carbohydrate.

- 20–30 g sugar
- 1 litre warm water
- 1–1.5 g salt
- Sugar-free squash for flavour

or

- 100 ml ordinary fruit squash
- 900 ml water
- 1–1.5 g salt

or

- 250 ml unsweetened fruit juice
- 750 ml water
- 1–1.5 g salt

To sum up ...

- Fluid consumption is vital during training and matches as well as at rest.

- Form a plan for fluid intake. Don't leave it to chance – always take a full drinks bottle to training and matches.

- Always start training/matches well hydrated, and drink little and often throughout.

- Remember thirst is a poor indicator of fluid needs – drink *before* you get thirsty.

- Drink during scheduled breaks in training/matches or in ad hoc breaks (e.g. when there are stoppages for injuries or penalties).

- Practise drinking during training – never try a new drink or drinking strategy during a match.

- Choose a drink you like the taste of and can afford.

- Fully rehydrate between training sessions and matches.

- Remember your dental health too – sports drinks contain sugar and can contribute to tooth decay. (For this reason never drink anything other than water after you clean your teeth at night. Even the weakest drink or milk will promote decay while you sleep.)

- Monitoring morning body weight is a good way to pick up on chronic dehydration.

Alcohol

The typical post-match diet will invariably include alcohol at some point. The issue with alcohol is how to ensure that it has as small an impact as possible on your subsequent training and matches. Most nutrition-related textbooks will warn you off alcohol but, in reality, most sports people will have a drink or two (or maybe ten) at some point during the week – it's how you cope with it that is the important factor.

The post-match pub visit is customary in many teams, but there are ways in which you can limit the effects of alcohol on your subsequent training and performance. After matches/training your alcohol intake should not interfere with your rehydration and refuelling needs.

- Remember that alcohol is not good for replacing the fluid lost from the body during a match or training. In fact, it is a diuretic (it makes you lose water) and will serve to dehydrate you further.

- Regardless of what the urban myth says, alcohol is not a way to 'carbo-load' or refuel, and alcoholic drinks will not contribute to your carbohydrate stores – they may even impair glycogen synthesis and so reduce energy levels. The calories in alcoholic drinks come from the alcohol itself not from carbohydrate.

However, even if you have rehydrated and refuelled, there is another reason why you should think carefully about the amount you drink after a match. Alcohol has a vasodilatory effect (it widens blood vessels) and this can cause extra swelling and bleeding in any damaged tissue. This will delay recovery and may also cause further damage to the injured area. For injured players, the most sensible thing to do is to avoid alcohol for 24–48 hours and celebrate (or commiserate) a day or two late.

How harmful is the occasional drinking binge?

You are not going to like this ...

Unfortunately, even a single drinking session will cause some sort of damage. As explained above, it will delay recovery; in addition to this, it will cause impairment of the following factors (and these effects may last up to 14 hours):

- balance
- reaction time
- co-ordination
- skill performance
- mental capacity.

Add this to the headaches, nausea, fatigue and dehydration associated with a hangover and this could crucially affect your next match/training session

Another factor to take into account, if body weight is an issue for you, is that alcohol has around 7 kcal/g and is therefore quite energy-dense. So, a good night out can add thousands of calories to your energy intake, and that's before we take into account the kebabs and curries.

The following list defines the body's reactions to alcohol.

- After just a couple of drinks the appetite is stimulated because alcohol triggers an increase in the gastric juices in the stomach.
- This fools the stomach into thinking that food is on its way when it isn't.
- This leads to hunger pangs – staunched, perhaps, with a few packets of crisps.
- After three to five drinks, the hunger wears off as the sugar content of the alcohol causes blood sugar levels to even out, reducing the craving for food.
- Additionally, the calories in the alcohol supply fuel, further reducing hunger pangs.
- However, after five or more drinks, an overload in sugar from the alcohol makes the body produce insulin, which results in a crash in blood sugar levels.

- Consequently, the cravings return even more intensely and if you don't eat at this stage you will begin to get irritable and angry. This is the point where anything you eat will taste good ... even that dodgy kebab!

The table on page 170 of the Appendix details the calorific content of some common alcoholic drinks.

How to improve your diet without becoming a monk

OK, so we've given you the bad news, and you've found out that your diet is a closer match to that of the late Oliver Reed (before he passed away, of course) than a finely tuned athlete. What can you *realistically* do about it, remembering that you will not always have access to, or the desire for, steamed fish and broccoli for every meal? Well, if you are in need of some suggestions, here they are.

Easy ways to cut calories and fat

Or 'How to cut 100 calories from your diet without really trying'.

Each of the suggestions in Table 5.2 will enable you to cut at least 100 calories out of your diet.

TABLE 5.2 Calorie-cutting changes

Change from	Change to
Sugar-free muesli, whole milk (250 kcal)	All-Bran, semi-skimmed milk (150 kcal)
2 scrambled eggs, milk and butter (296 kcal)	2 poached eggs (147 kcal)
2 grilled pork sausages (254 kcal)	2 grilled rashers of lean bacon (146 kcal)
1 freshly baked croissant (216 kcal)	2 slices of toast from a small loaf (116 kcal)
2 pats of real butter (144 kcal)	2 tbsps of raspberry jam (42 kcal)
150 g of Greek yoghurt (240 kcal)	150 g low-fat plain yoghurt (84 kcal)
1 beef and horseradish sandwich (347 kcal)	1 lean ham and mustard sandwich (243 kcal)
1 egg mayonnaise sandwich (641 kcal)	1 egg salad sandwich (401 kcal)
1 bowl of cream of tomato soup (165 kcal)	1 bowl of gazpacho (60 kcal)
1 baked potato, butter and cheese (409 kcal)	1 baked potato with baked beans (265 kcal)

TABLE 5.2 Calorie-cutting changes – continued

Change from	Change to
1 rounded tbsp of mayonnaise (139 kcal)	1 tbsp of salsa (20 kcal)
2 fresh bagels (402 kcal)	2 fresh wholemeal rolls (230 kcal)
1 portion of spaghetti carbonara (539 kcal)	1 portion of spaghetti Neapolitan (339 kcal)
150 g of chip-shop chips (358 kcal)	150 g of supermarket oven chips (250 kcal)
2 grilled lamb chops (664 kcal)	8 oz grilled rump steak (436 kcal)
1 chicken breast with skin (302 kcal)	1 lean turkey breast (194 kcal)
1 plate of chicken korma (660 kcal)	1 plate of chicken piri-piri (375 kcal)
1 steamed salmon steak (360 kcal)	2 grilled fishcakes (197 kcal)
1 Mars bar (287 kcal)	1 Flake bar (180 kcal)
3 chocolate digestive biscuits (222 kcal)	3 Jaffa Cakes (109 kcal)
50 g bag of salted peanuts (301 kcal)	50 g of Twiglets (192 kcal)
4 fresh figs (167 kcal)	20 fresh cherries (38 kcal)
2 bananas, small bunch of grapes (155 kcal)	1 slice of melon, 1 kiwi (49 kcal)
1 Magnum ice cream (287 kcal)	1 Solero ice cream (125 kcal)
3 cups of tea, sugar and semi-skimmed milk (158 kcal)	3 cups of tea, no sugar, skimmed milk (40 kcal)
1 glass of Baileys Irish Cream (150 kcal)	1 glass of Scotch whisky (50 kcal)
300 ml glass whole milk (204 kcal)	300 ml glass of semi-skimmed milk (102 kcal)
1 can of Coca-Cola (128 kcal)	1 can of Diet Coca-Cola (2 kcal)
1 mug of drinking chocolate with semi-skimmed milk (178 kcal)	1 cup of Options hot chocolate with water (40 kcal)
half pint of vintage cider (286 kcal)	half pint of Guinness (105 kcal)

Fast food and fitness

Nobody playing outside the professional ranks is likely to avoid the odd slip. This book is about balance, so it will be useful for you to know what you can eat that won't wreck the hard training you have done.

You will notice that I haven't included the well-known burger and chicken outlets in the following pages – if you want to know about them why not take a look in the Appendix to see what wholesome effect (not!) they are likely to have on you.

General tips

Here are some guidelines to follow when eating out. The key here is just to understand the principles and be moderate in your choices.

- Choose meals that aren't fried – ask for grilled meat and/or fish.

- Choose tomato-based sauces not cream-based ones.

- Choose jacket potatoes or boiled potatoes as an alternative to chips or sauté potatoes.

- Eat plenty of salad, vegetables and fruit.

- Try to eat high-carbohydrate food choices such as pasta, rice or pizza (deep pan) instead of high-fat foods, and have extra bread with your meal.

- Choose desserts such as fruit, low-fat ice cream, sorbets, yoghurt and fromage frais.

Indian food
LOWER FAT

- **Starters**
  Tikka or tandoori, sheesh kebab, tandoori grill, dokhala (daal), Bombay mix, poppadoms and chutneys

- **Main courses**
  Dupiaza, bhoona, jalfrezi, rogan josh, dhansak, original balti sauces or tandoori kebabs, biryani, thali

- **Side orders**
  Aloo gobi, Bombay potatoes, pnar and spinach, daal, raitha, tarka daal (lentil sauce), bhindi, channa (chickpeas) and sag (spinach); boiled, basmati and mushroom rice dishes; original naan and chapatti breads

- **Desserts**
  Fresh fruit, sorbet, ice cream, lassi and kulfi

HIGHER FAT

- **Starters**
  Samosas, bhajis, aloo vadhal, crispy rolls, pakora, curry patties, wada and prawn puri

- **Main courses**
  Massalla, korma and pasanda dishes

- **Side orders**
  Daal massalla, pakoras, bhajis, special fried rice, egg fried rice, keema rice; keema, peshwari and garlic naans, paratha and puri (fried) breads

- **Desserts**
  Apple and banana fritters, kheer and jallebi

Mexican
LOWER FAT

- **Starters**
  Bean soup, buffalo wings, guacamole dip and taco salad

- **Main courses**
  Burritos, enchiladas, fajitas, tacos, chili con carne, kebabs, paella

- **Side orders**
  Jacket potatoes, corn tortillas, rice, guacamole and salad

- **Desserts**
  Fresh fruit, ice cream, sorbets

HIGHER FAT

- **Starters**
  Nachos with cheese, stuffed garlic mushrooms, deep-fried potato skins

- **Main courses**
  Chimichangas, hamburgers, fries

- **Side orders**
  French fries, fried onions, fried mushrooms, garlic bread with cheese, refried beans, salad dressings, sour cream
- **Desserts**
  Cheesecake, pecan pie etc. with cream

Italian
LOWER FAT

- **Starters**
  Bread sticks, ciabatta, focaccia, corn on the cob, vegetable or minestrone soup, pate with toast, parma ham with melon, meatballs in tomato sauce

- **Main courses**
  Napolitana, bolognese, pizzaiola, puttanesca, primavera, vongole, funghi, prosciutto, all'arrabbiata and provencale sauces, pizza (deep pan)

- **Desserts**
  Fresh fruit salad, ice cream, sorbet, pancakes with fruit, cheese and biscuits

HIGHER FAT

- **Starters**
  Deep-fried whitebait or squid, garlic mushrooms, garlic bread

- **Main courses**
  Carbonara, gamberetti and any other creamy sauces

- **Desserts**
  Tiramisu, Italian gateau, zabaglione, cheesecake

Chinese

LOWER FAT

- **Starters**
  Soups, meat or fish satay dip, aromatic duck with pancakes, lettuce wraps, prawn crackers

- **Main courses**
  Chow mein, chop suey or foo yung dishes, bean sprout, chilli, oyster, yellow, sweet and sour or black bean sauces, curries

- **Side orders**
  Stir-fried Chinese veg, noodles and salads, boiled rice

- **Desserts**
  Fresh fruit, lychees, sorbet, ice cream, toffee banana/apple

HIGHER FAT

- **Starters**
  Spare ribs, spring rolls, sesame prawn toast, crispy seaweed, fried bean curd

- **Main courses**
  Food served in batter, satay sauce, fried rice

- **Side orders**
  Fried veg, battered veg, special fried rice, prawn fried rice

- **Desserts**
  Apple, banana and pineapple fritters

Wonder supplements

You must make up your own mind about supplements, but you'll get most of what you want from a proper balanced diet.

There are plenty of super-duper supplements available on the market that make all sorts of spurious claims. I recommend that you follow the rule 'If it's too good to be true, it probably is.' There are times and instances when it may be appropriate to use a supplement but don't fall into the trap of believing that they can take the place of proper physical preparation.

Stirring creatine powder into your third pint of lager after a training session really isn't going to have any positive effect. If you are honest with yourself and you have read the previous pages you will know what *will* make a change and what is just 'window dressing'. However, described below are a few of the more regularly used supplements and a little bit about them.

Glucosamine

Glucosamine is one of the fastest-growing nutritional supplements on the market at the moment and is becoming increasingly well known for its varied benefits. Its popularity has boomed after it was successfully used to relieve symptoms in osteoarthritis patients. But will it work for sports people? The claimed benefits of glucosamine supplementation include speedier recovery from connective tissue (ligament/tendon) injuries, reduced joint pain, increased joint lubrication and reduced inflammation.

What is it?

Glucosamine sulphate (the type used in most supplements) is a naturally occurring substance that is found in large quantities in the body, but mainly in the cartilage and synovial fluid (a lubricating agent found in joints).

What does it do?

Supplementation with glucosamine will, it is said, enhance the body's ability to manufacture the elements that are essential to the process of rebuilding damaged joint structures. It is also thought that it will be able to enhance the manufacture of fluids that enhance the lubrication of, and shock absorption within, joints. In addition, it appears to act as an anti-inflammatory, and research has indicated that it may act as a preventative measure against osteoarthritis.

The argument for

It is believed that the benefits of glucosamine supplementation in sport will mainly arise from its ability to regenerate cartilage, and aid joint lubrication and shock absorption. Also, the anti-inflammatory effects of glucosamine have been proposed as being beneficial to the sporting community. When you consider the amount of overuse injuries and joint injuries that occur in sport, it follows that anything that can help to ease pain and speed recovery will be of benefit.

Recommended dosage

The recommended dosage for glucosamine is 1,500 mg per day, which can be taken as one 1,500 mg dose, two 750 mg doses or three 500 mg doses. Be aware, however, that the effects of glucosamine normally take about four weeks to become apparent – it is not an instant-action supplement. Glucosamine is extremely well tolerated and there are no known contra-indications or adverse interactions with drugs. However, in rare cases, it may cause some gastro-intestinal upset (e.g. nausea). If this does occur, try taking it with meals.

Creatine

Scientific evidence suggests that short-term creatine supplementation can improve performance during repeated high-intensity exercise; therefore, it seems that it should be beneficial for tennis performance. Creatine is possibly the only 'effective' ergogenic aid that does not contravene International Olympic Committee (IOC) doping regulations and, as such, it would be inappropriate not to make its use an option to those athletes that may find it beneficial.

Current scientific thinking views short-term creatine supplementation as a safe, effective and legal ergogenic aid. However, recent reports (highlighted in the media) have questioned both the safety and ethics of its use. These issues are discussed below to enable you to make an informed decision regarding its use.

What does it do?

Here comes the science bit ...

Energy for muscle action is supplied by a substance called adenosine triphosphate (ATP). When ATP is broken down, energy is released. However, muscles can only store enough ATP to perform high-intensity muscle actions for about 10 seconds, and they will fatigue if ATP levels drop below 25–30 per cent of the normal level. So, you need to maintain ATP levels if you want to continue to exercise at the same intensity.

The theory behind supplementing with creatine is that it increases the availability of phosphocreatine in the muscles, which may enhance energy provision during brief, high-intensity exercise. It may also increase the phosphocreatine stores within muscles, allowing a faster rate of ATP regeneration both during and after high-intensity exercise.

The argument for

Scientific evidence suggests that short-term creatine supplementation can improve performance during repeated high-intensity exercise. Current thinking views short-term supplementation as a safe, effective and legal aid to performance.

LONG-TERM SIDE-EFFECTS

Creatine is still a relatively new supplement, even though it is one of the most popular and most celebrated. Therefore, even though investigations are being carried out into the effects of long-term, high-dosage use, it has not been around long enough for scientists/doctors to say that it is safe to use for long periods of time. Unfortunately, there is no knowing whether taking large doses of creatine for long periods will cause any unwanted side-effects in the future.

However, based on current data, and the informed decisions of doctors and sports scientists, creatine appears to be a safe and effective performance enhancer, as long as it is taken in the way recommended. Any risks associated with the long-term usage of creatine are linked to the ingestion of large volumes of creatine for sustained periods.

LEGALITY

As creatine is found in meat eaters' diets, it would be difficult to determine where excess amounts were being ingested from. Therefore it is not currently in violation of any sports governing body's rules. Additionally, the IOC, as mentioned above, does not include creatine on its list of banned substances.

Protein supplements

For many years experts, coaches and competitors have debated the question of whether or not athletes – particularly those trying to gain muscle mass – should consume extraordinary amounts of protein in their diets. There are literally hundreds of protein supplements on the market and they consistently hold their place among the top sellers. But are the millions of pounds handed over for these products being spent wisely or just 'peed down the pan'?

What are they?

Protein is essential for all life. It comprises about 15 per cent of the body weight of a human and is found primarily in muscle. Although there are many different proteins, they are all made up of amino acids. Our bodies can make proteins from amino acids but they can only produce some of the necessary amino acids. Those that cannot be made in the body must be obtained from the diet.

What do they do?

Protein is essential for growth and is used within the body to build new tissue and replace old, worn-out tissue such as muscles. Although protein can be used as an energy source, the actual contribution to overall energy production is normally very small. During short-duration exercise (sprinting, weightlifting) the contribution from protein is negligible, regardless of the intensity of the exercise. Longer-duration exercise (distance running, cycling) may be partially fuelled by protein, but the contribution is still small at approximately 2–5 per cent. However, there are situations when the energy contribution may be higher; these include times when carbohydrate stores are low. Even in such cases, however, the contribution of protein is probably 10 per cent at most.

The argument for

Regular exercise and training may increase protein needs, the extent to which this occurs being dependent on the type and duration of the exercise undertaken. Protein supplements are generally marketed at the athlete who is trying to increase muscle mass and therefore undertaking a certain amount of resistance training. When attempts are made to increase muscle mass, additional protein may be required to provide sufficient amino acids to maximise protein synthesis. Several scientific studies have concluded that resistance exercise does, indeed, increase protein synthesis, suggesting a need for extra protein in the diet.

Other studies have tried to quantify the actual amount of protein that would be required by strength training athletes in order to optimise muscle growth. One study, in the early 1990s, reported that when 2 g/kg of protein was consumed each day for four weeks, whole-body protein synthesis increased and significantly more lean mass was achieved than in subjects who consumed their normal diet. So, this evidence seems to point towards strength trained athletes needing more protein in their diets.

The argument against

However, the same study also found an increase in amino acid oxidation, which suggests that the protein intake of 2 g/kg per day actually exceeded the amount that was needed for muscle growth. A separate study supported this by reporting that a protein intake of 2.4 g/kg per day did not increase protein synthesis more than an intake of 1.4 g/kg per day, but the larger intake did increase amino acid oxidation. Therefore, the extra intake was not being used for increasing muscle mass.

The recommendations for protein intake by athletes is generally between 1.2 and 1.8 g/kg per day. However, a beginner may need slightly more in the first couple of weeks. The only athletes who realistically need more than this are children and adolescents, who need extra protein to allow for growth and may need up to 2 g/kg per day. Most athletes will meet their protein needs through their diets, although people following energy-restriction diets or strict vegetarian diets may need to address their protein intake. One recommendation for athletes who believe they are not consuming adequate protein is dry milk powder (casein), which will provide all the necessary amino acids at a fraction of the cost of protein supplements. There is simply no scientific evidence to suggest that the protein in supplements is more effective for athletes than protein in ordinary foods.

Where do they occur naturally?

Protein is found in many foods such as dairy products, fish, meat, poultry, soya products, meat substitutes (such as Quorn), beans, nuts, bread and cereals. However, a lot of these foods tend to be high in fat or cooked in ways that increase fat content, so be careful if you are watching your weight!

Thermogenic aids/fat burners
What are they?

Supplements that will apparently help you to lose body weight effortlessly. The word 'thermogenic' literally means 'to produce heat', and something that causes you to burn more calories is said to have a thermogenic effect. These supplements often contain stimulants such as caffeine, ephedrine or guarana. Other supplements touted as 'fat burners' contain substances like carnitine, chromium and pyruvate.

What do they do?

These substances claim to metabolise fat and use it as a fuel source so draining your fat stores and making you leaner! Some of these supplements may be helpful in suppressing appetite and controlling food cravings. Stimulant-type supplements are responsible for decreasing your appetite and increasing your calorie utilisation over a short period of time. However, they do nothing to affect your basal metabolic rate (BMR), which is the amount of calories you use at rest.

The argument for

Although a combination of sensible dieting and exercise is known to be the most effective way to reduce body fat, the thought that 'popping a few pills' may help you do it faster can be very alluring. None of these supplements, however, is able to simply melt away your fat deposits.

Stimulant substances function to slightly increase energy expenditure and suppress appetite, and have been shown to reduce weight in obese subjects. Examples of substances tested include caffeine, guarana and ephedra. Guarana is found in many weight loss products, while ephedra is present in almost all 'fat-burning' products; both of these are naturally occurring, herbal equivalents of caffeine and therefore act on the central nervous system to elicit the effects described above. However, both have also been linked with the side-effects detailed below.

Chromium is one of the most popular supplements used for weight loss. It plays a vital role in carbohydrate metabolism and may help control blood sugar levels, so helping to reduce cravings. Pyruvate is another supplement commonly associated with weight loss as it may enhance the amount of fat lost while following a calorie-controlled diet. This seems to be due to its ability to slightly increase the metabolic rate and, hence, the number of calories used per day while consuming it.

Carnitine is a supplement that does have some scientific backing to its claims. Human muscles contain a large amount of carnitine and its primary function is to transport fat to the sites in the muscles where it can be used for energy. So, the theory is that if you increase the amount of carnitine in the muscle you will increase the amount of fat being used and so start to drain your fat stores.

The argument against

In reality, there is no magic pill or powder that will accelerate body fat loss. Few nutritional supplements that are advertised as able to 'burn fat' have ever been proven to do so. In fact, the only true thermogenic aids are water, oxygen, exercise and proper nutrition.

Only two – chromium and pyruvate – have undergone rigorous scientific scrutiny, and this was in obese subjects not athletes. Other studies show that carnitine has no effect on body fat, fat metabolism or performance; there are also those that show positive effects. In fact, studies have shown that the carnitine molecules ingested as supplements are too large to be able to enter the muscle cell anyway, so they are completely ineffective!

Ephedrine is a banned substance and a drug rather than a nutritional supplement. However, it occurs naturally in many herbal products such as ephedra (e.g. Ma Huang and Chinese Ephedra), mentioned above. Ephedrine has a structure similar to that of amphetamines and there is no data on its ability to reduce weight in healthy, non-obese individuals. It can cause side-effects such as tremors and nervousness, and can also increase heart rate and blood pressure. Even more serious side-effects that have been reported include myocardial infarctions, strokes, seizures, psychosis and death. Combining ephedrine with other stimulants, such as caffeine, increases the potency of the stimulant and the chances of adverse events. Long-term stimulant use can also depress your BMR, meaning that you are more likely to end up gaining weight rather than losing it, due to the following factors.

- **Dehydration** – stimulants have a diuretic effect, which increases the risk of dehydration and inhibits fat metabolism.

- **Muscle breakdown** – restricting calories and using stimulants increases the production of stress hormones, which convert muscle tissue into glucose to raise blood sugar levels. Reducing muscle mass effectively lowers the BMR and increases the risk of fatigue, injury and illness.

- **Poor performance** – elevated stress levels and broken-down muscle tissue result in poor performance and a reduced ability to exercise, which will result in a further drop in the BMR.

Recipe and snack ideas

Moving away from all the talk of supplements, let's get back to more 'natural' dietary concerns. Here are some ideas for quick, easy and nutritious (and sometimes portable) snacks.

Sandwiches

Sandwiches are a convenient component of packed meals to take to school or college, and indeed to training and competitions. All breads are an excellent source of carbohydrate. When making sandwiches, use a small amount of low-fat spread. Avoid using spread at all with moist sandwich fillings.

Serving suggestions

- Tri-wedges – include a third slice of bread in the centre of the sandwich
- Toast wedges – toast the bread to make a hot snack or use a sandwich maker
- Pocket wedges – filled pitta breads
- Roll wedges – place fillings on naan breads and roll up
- Continental wedges – try different breads such as rye, pumpernickel, bagels and bread sticks
- Cut slices of bread thickly

Filling ideas

- Lean roast meat with pickle, mustard and chutney with salad
- Cooked chicken or turkey with reduced-fat mayo or cranberry sauce – add mixed salad and chopped walnuts
- Reduced-fat cheese and lean ham – add celery, lettuce, grated carrot and/or tomato
- Cottage or ricotta cheese with dried fruit, chopped walnuts and mixed salad
- Low-fat humus with cucumber and grated carrot
- Tuna in brine or salmon with salad, spring onions or cucumber

- Marmite with cottage cheese and salad
- Cottage cheese with fruit
- Ham, cottage or ricotta cheese and pineapple
- Banana and raisin
- Low-fat pate, salmon or tuna paste
- Low-fat cream cheese and tomato
- Grilled bacon, lettuce and tomato
- Chopped chicken and sweetcorn with low-calorie dressing

Toppings for toast, muffins, bagels and crumpets

- Spaghetti, baked beans or tinned ravioli
- Jam, syrup or honey
- Grilled low-fat cheese and pineapple
- Mashed banana and cinnamon
- Low-fat cheese and lean ham
- Scrambled egg and tomato sauce
- Low-fat cream cheese and banana
- Chopped egg mixed with plain yoghurt
- Sardines/mackerel in tomato sauce

Desserts

- Fresh or tinned fruits
- Low-fat yoghurt or fromage frais
- Low-fat tinned or home-made rice pudding or custard
- Low-fat mousse
- Low-fat ice cream
- Sorbet
- Jelly

Baked potato fillings

- Mexican tuna – tinned tomatoes, red pepper, onion and tuna
- Cheesy bean potatoes – baked beans, low-fat grated cheese and pepper
- Mushroom toppers – onion, mushroom, tomato, basil and black pepper
- Mushroom and beans – sliced mushrooms, onions and baked beans
- Chicken and sweetcorn – cooked chicken, sweetcorn, fromage frais, mustard, pepper and parsley
- Fishy potato – tinned fish in tomato sauce, chopped pepper and tomato
- Bacon delight – lean grilled bacon, grilled mushrooms and tomatoes

More potato ideas

- New potato salad – new potatoes in natural yoghurt with spring onions and sweetcorn
- Minted potato salad – new potatoes in low-fat yoghurt, garlic, cucumber and mint
- Hot potato salad – boiled new potatoes in low-fat yoghurt, garlic, onion, wholegrain mustard, curry paste; sprinkle with a little low-fat grated cheese and bake until hot throughout

AFTERWORD

I hope that the information in this pack makes sense to you and will help you to realise whatever goals you set yourself. To summarise the key elements that make up the core of your programme, they are as follows.

Plan ...

... carefully and set realistic objectives for yourself.

Review ...

... constantly by maintaining your progress chart. If you have reached a plateau then it is time to change your routine.

Observe ...

... others at work and yourself to ensure that proper form is maintained.

Communicate

Tell someone close to you what you are up to and involve him or her in the project to help you in the low times that are sure to come.

Enjoy

It is OK to enjoy yourself. Be proud of what you achieve and take it on to the field with you so that you can get the most out of your tennis.

APPENDIX: FOOD AND DRINK DATA

TABLE A.1 The calorific content of alcoholic drinks

Drink	Quantity	Calories
BEERS/LAGERS		
Amstel	1 pint	165
Becks	1 bottle (12 oz/340 ml)	145
Budweiser	1 bottle (12 oz/340 ml)	135
Budweiser Light	1 bottle (12 oz/340 ml)	100
Carling Black Label	1 pint	256
Coors	1 pint	220
Coors Light	1 pint	170
Fosters	1 pint	240
Grolsch	1 bottle (12 oz/340 ml)	150
Guinness	1 pint	245
Harp	1 pint	227
Heineken	1 pint	265
Kronenburg	1 pint	245
Lowenbrau	1 bottle (12 oz/340 ml)	155
Miller	1 bottle (12 oz/340 ml)	140
Miller Lite	1 bottle (12 oz/340 ml)	105
Pilsner	1 bottle (12 oz/340 ml)	155
Red Stripe	1 pint	245
Rolling Rock Premium	1 bottle (12 oz/340 ml)	120
WINES		
Champagne	1 glass (4 oz/110 ml)	85
Dry white	1 glass (4 oz/110 ml)	75
Sweet white	1 glass (4 oz/110 ml)	105
Red	1 glass (4 oz/110 ml)	80
SPIRITS/LIQUEURS		
Baileys	1 measure (37.5 ml)	115
Brandy	1 shot (1 oz/30 ml)	65
Cointreau	1 shot (1.5 oz/45 ml)	190
Drambuie	1 shot (1.5 oz/45 ml)	190
Gin	1 shot (1 oz/30 ml)	65
Rum	1 shot (1 oz/30 ml)	65
Tequila	1 shot (1 oz/30 ml)	65
Vodka	1 shot (1 oz/30 ml)	65
Whisky	1 shot (1 oz/30 ml)	65

TABLE A.2 What 50 g of carbohydrate looks like*

Food	50 g serving	Food	50 g serving
Fruit juice	1 pint	Pitta bread	2
Full sugar fruit squash	3 glasses	Ryvita	9
Milk	2 pints	Crispbreads	15 small/6 large
Flavoured milk	1 pint	Rice cakes	6 thick/10 thin
Soft drinks	1 pint	Cereal bars	3
3% carbohydrate drink	1670 ml	Muesli bars	2.5
6% carbohydrate drink	833 ml	Malt loaf	3 slices
7.5% carbohydrate drink	666 ml	Sweetcorn	10 tbsps/2 cbs
Fruit in heavy syrup	1 small tin	Baked potatoes	1 large
Fruit in juice	1 large tin	Ravioli	8 tbsps
Apples	4	Rice (boiled)	4 tbsps
Oranges	4	Pasta	8 tbsps
Bananas	2	Noodles	8 tbsps
Pears	3	Tinned spaghetti in	
		tomato sauce	8 tbsps/1 large can
Dried apricots	20	Baked beans	7 tbsps/1 large can
Raisins	4 tbsps	Rice (fried)	6 tbsps
Bran flakes	1 large bowl	Pizza	0.25 deep pan
Weetabix	5 biscuits	Fromage frais	2 tubs
Cornflakes	1 large bowl	Low-fat fruit yoghurt	2 pots
Muesli	1 medium bowl	Plain sweet biscuits	9
Bagels	1	Jaffa cakes	6
Bread	4 slices	Jam/marmalade	9 tsps
Crumpets	3	Honey/syrup	9 tsps
English muffins	2	Fruit pastilles	2 tubes
Croissants	2	Jelly babies	1 medium packet (60 g)
Bread rolls	2	Iced fruit bun	1.5

* Table of foods and the portion sizes needed to provide 50 g of carbohydrate

TABLE A.3 What 10 g of protein looks like*

Food	10 g serving	Food	10 g serving
Grilled fish	50 g (cooked weight)	Cottage cheese	70 g
Tuna/salmon	50 g	Semi-skimmed milk	300 ml
Lean beef/lamb	35 g (cooked weight)	Muesli	1 cup (100 g)
Veal	35 g (cooked weight)	Wholemeal bread	4 slices (120 g)
Turkey/chicken	40 g (cooked weight)	Cooked brown rice	3 cups (400 g)
Eggs	2 small	Cooked lentils	0.75 cup (150 g)
Low-fat fromage frais	150 g	Cooked kidney beans	0.75 cup (150 g)
Reduced-fat cheese	30 g	Baked beans	1 small can (200 g)
Low-fat yoghurt	200 g	Tofu	120 g
Seeds (i.e. sesame)	60 g	Nuts	60 g
Wheat bran flake cereal	3 cups (90 g)	Cooked pasta/noodles	2 cups (300 g)

* Table of foods and the portion sizes needed to provide 10 g of protein

Fast-food hell?

It is one of God's little jests that lots of the stuff that tastes great is not much benefit to us. Check out the following stats on fast-food values.

TABLE A.4 Fast-food hell?

Product	Calories	Fat (g)	Carbs (g)	Protein (g)
McDONALD'S				
Hamburger	260	9	34	13
Cheeseburger	320	13	35	15
Quarter Pounder	420	21	37	23
Quarter Pounder w/Cheese	530	30	38	28
Big Mac	560	31	45	26
Crispy Chicken Deluxe	500	25	43	26
Fish Fillet Deluxe	560	28	54	23
Grilled Chicken Deluxe	440	20	38	27
Small Fries	210	10	26	3

TABLE A.4 Fast-food hell? – continued

Product	Calories	Fat (g)	Carbs (g)	Protein (g)
Large Fries	450	22	57	6
Super Fries	540	26	68	8
Chicken McNuggets (4)	190	11	10	12
Chicken McNuggets (6)	290	17	15	18
Chicken McNuggets (9)	430	26	23	27
Hot Mustard	60	3.5	7	1
Honey Mustard	50	4.5	3	0
Light Mayonnaise	40	4	0	0
Garden Salad	35	0	7	2
Grilled Chicken Salad Deluxe	120	1.5	7	21
Croutons	50	1.5	7	2
Caesar Salad	160	14	7	2
Ranch Dressing	230	21	10	1
Egg McMuffin	290	12	27	17
Sausage McMuffin	360	23	26	13
Sausage & Egg McMuffin	440	28	27	19
English Muffin	140	2	25	4
Sausage	170	16	0	6
Scrambled Eggs (2)	160	11	1	13
Hash Browns	130	8	14	1
Pancakes Plain	310	7	53	9
Pancakes w/Margarine and Syrup	580	16	100	9
Apple Danish	360	16	51	5
Cinnamon Roll	400	20	47	7
Strawberry Sundae	290	7	50	7
Hot Caramel Sundae	360	10	61	7
Baked Apple Pie	260	13	34	3
Chocolate Chip Cookie	170	10	22	2
McDonald's Cookies	180	5	32	3
Vanilla Shake (small)	360	9	59	11
Chocolate Shake (small)	360	9	60	11
Strawberry Shake (small)	360	9	60	11
Orange Juice	80	0	20	1
Coca-Cola (small)	150	0	40	0
Coca-Cola (medium)	210	0	58	0
Coca-Cola (large)	310	0	86	0
Diet Coke (any size)	0	0	0	0

TABLE A.4 Fast-food hell? – continued

Product	Calories	Fat (g)	Carbs (g)	Protein (g)
Sprite (small)	150	0	39	0
Sprite (medium)	210	0	56	0
Sprite (large)	310	0	83	0
BURGER KING				
Whopper Sandwich	640	39	45	27
Whopper Sandwich with Cheese	730	46	46	33
Double Whopper	870	56	45	46
Double Whopper with Cheese	960	63	46	52
Whopper Jr	420	24	29	21
Whopper Jr with Cheese	460	28	29	23
Hamburger	330	15	28	20
Cheeseburger	380	19	28	23
Double Cheeseburger	600	36	28	41
Double Cheeseburger + Bacon	640	39	28	44
BK Big Fish	700	41	56	26
BK Broiler	550	29	41	30
Chicken Sandwich	710	43	54	26
Chicken Tenders (8 pieces)	310	17	19	21
Broiled Chicken Salad	200	10	7	21
Garden Salad no dressing	100	5	7	6
Side Salad no dressing	60	3	4	3
French Fries (medium/salted)	370	20	43	5
Coated French Fries	340	17	43	0
Onion Rings	310	14	41	4
Dutch Apple Pie	300	15	39	3
Vanilla Shake (medium)	300	6	53	9
Chocolate Shake (medium)	320	7	54	9
Coca Cola Classic (medium)	280	0	70	0
Diet Coke (medium)	1	0	0	0
Sprite (medium)	260	0	66	0
Tropicana Orange Juice	140	0	33	2
Coffee	5	0	1	0
Milk (2% low fat)	130	5	12	8
Croissant w/Sausage, Egg, Cheese	600	46	25	22
Hash Browns	220	12	25	2
Lettuce	0	0	0	0

TABLE A.4 Fast-food hell? – continued

Product	Calories	Fat (g)	Carbs (g)	Protein (g)
Tomato	5	0	1	0
Onion	5	0	1	0
Pickles	0	0	0	0
Ketchup	15	0	4	0
Mustard	0	0	0	0
Mayonnaise	210	23	0	0
Tartar Sauce	180	19	0	0
Bull's Eye BBQ Sauce	20	0	5	0
Bacon Bits	15	1	0	1
Croutons	30	1	4	0
1000 Island Dressing	140	12	7	0
French Dressing	140	10	11	0
Ranch Dressing	180	19	2	0
Blue Cheese Dressing	160	16	1	2
Honey	90	0	23	0
BBQ Sauce	35	0	9	0
Sweet/Sour Sauce	45	0	11	0
DOMINO'S PIZZA				
Thin Crust Cheese (one-sixth)	255	11	28	11
Deep Dish Cheese (one-sixth)	463	20	55	18
Thin Crust w/Peppers, olives, mushrooms (one-sixth)	271	12	29	12
Deep Dish w/peppers, olives, mushrooms (one-sixth)	480	21	56	19
Thin Crust Pepperoni (one-sixth)	354	19	30	16
Deep Dish Pepperoni (one-sixth)	563	28	56	23
Thin Crust Cheese (one-quarter)	273	12	30	12
Deep Dish Cheese (one-quarter)	467	21	52	18
Cheese Pizza (1 pizza)	591	27	65	23
Barbecque Wings (1)	50	2	2	6
Hot Wings (1)	45	2	1	5
Breadsticks (1)	78	3	11	2
Cheesy Bread (1)	103	5	11	3
Small Garden Salad	22	0	4	1
Large Garden Salad	39	0	8	2

TABLE A.4 Fast-food hell? – continued

Product	Calories	Fat (g)	Carbs (g)	Protein (g)
KFC				
Wing with skin	121	8	1	12
Breast with skin	251	11	1	37
Breast without skin	169	4	1	31
Thigh with skin	207	12	2	18
Thigh without skin	106	6	1	13
Drumstick with skin	97	4	1	15
Drumstick without skin	67	2	1	11
Whole wing	140	10	5	9
Crispy Strips (3)	261	16	10	20
Chunky Chicken Pot Pie	770	42	69	29
Hot Wings Pieces (6)	471	33	18	27
Original Recipe Chicken Sandwich	497	22	46	29
Value BBQ Chicken Sandwich	256	8	28	17
Kentucky Nuggets (6)	284	18	15	16
Corn on the Cob	190	3	34	5
Green Beans	45	2	7	1
BBQ Baked Beans	190	3	33	6
PIZZA HUT				
Thin 'N' Crispy (1 slice)	210	9	21	12
Pan (1 slice)	300	14	30	15
Stuffed Crust (1 slice)	380	11	49	21
Buffalo Wings mild (5)	200	12	0	23
Buffalo Wings hot (4)	210	12	4	22
Garlic Bread (1 slice)	150	8	16	3
Bread Stick (1 slice)	130	4	20	3
Bread Stick Dip Sauce	30	0.5	5	0
Spaghetti w/Marinara	490	6	91	18
Spaghetti w/Meat Sauce	600	13	98	23
Spaghetti w/Meatballs	850	24	120	37
Cavatini Pasta	480	14	66	21
Cavatini Supreme Pasta	560	19	73	24
Ham and Cheese Sandwich	550	21	57	33
Supreme Sandwich	640	28	62	34
Apple Dessert Pizza (1 slice)	250	4.5	48	3
Cherry Dessert Pizza (1 slice)	250	4.5	47	3

FURTHER READING

Arnold's Body Building For Men
Authors: Arnold Schwarzenegger and Bill Dobbins
Published by: Fireside; Reprint edition (October 12, 1984) **ISBN**: 0671531638
Summary: Ah, now you may be surprised that this finds its way into this book's selection of recommended reading. Surely Arnie is a musclebound poser? Think again – this book is packed full of good basic information. Surprisingly, protein shakes, supplements of dubious value, and exotic weight training routines are notable by their absence. Great book for dipping into.

Circuit Training
Authors: Morgan and Adamson
Published by: Bell **ISBN**: 0713507659
Summary: The first and still the best- from the *originators* of circuit training. Vital if you want all-over fitness

The Complete Guide to Strength Training 3rd edition
Author: Anita Bean
Published by: A & C Black **ISBN**: 0713660406
Summary: A great book if you have a little more time on your hands or just want some more variety. Be aware, though, that it has its basis in the bodybuilding and 'reshaping' world, whose objectives differ from those of this book.

Essentials of Strength Training and Conditioning
Authors: Baechle and Earle
Published by: Human Kinetics **ISBN**: 0873226941
Summary: The most comprehensive work ever written on this subject.

Food for Fitness
Author: Anita Bean
Published by: A & C Black **ISBN**: 0713663863
Summary: A good, practical guide. Covers topics such as eating on the run, boosting your energy, healthy snacks, healthy weight loss, and recipes such as snack bars and pasta.

The Inner Game of Tennis
Author: W.Timothy Gallwey
Published by: Pan **ISBN**: 0330295136
Summary: Not, strictly speaking, a book about physical sports conditioning. However, if you have ever wondered how you can address inconsistency, and how your mind and body fit together on a tennis court (and indeed in life generally) then this is the one!

Know The Game: Weightlifting, Powerlifting, Weight Training (three separate booklets)
Authors: Various
Published by: A & C Black **ISBN**: Various
Summary: Backed by the British Weightlifting Association. Ideal for the beginner. Three simple, clear introductions.

Sports Training Principles
Author: Frank Dick
Published by: A & C Black **ISBN**: 0713658657
Summary: Possibly the best book ever written on the subject – quite superb. An advanced version of the same author's *Training Theory* (see below).

Strength Training
Author: Max Jones
Published by: BAAB **ISBN**: 0851340970
Summary: Clear explanation and illustrations. A superb introduction – especially if you train alone.

Strength Training Anatomy
Author: Frederic Delavier
Published by: Human Kinetics **ISBN**: 0736041850
Summary: Full-colour illustrations of the muscles used during the exercises. Brilliant illustrations – the only drawback is that it is aimed at bodybuilders rather than athletes. Well worth a glance though and a very nice coffee table book.

Training Theory
Author: Frank Dick
Published by: BAAB **ISBN**: 0851341055
Summary: An excellent introduction to the ideas that govern training for fitness. If you want to understand what you are doing, this is for you.

The Weightlifting Encyclopedia: A Guide to World-Class Performance
Author: Arthur Drechsler
Published by: A is A Communications **ISBN**: 0965917924
Summary: This covers absolutely everything you could ever ask about Olympic lifting. If you are going to use O-lifts as a core part of your training then this is fabulous reading.

Weight Training and Lifting
Author: John Lear
Published by: A & C Black **ISBN**: 0713656743
Summary: The official British Weight Lifting Association Text. Excellent

Conrad Phillips runs individually tailored courses for clubs and individuals and can be contacted via *email: conrad.phillips@btinternet.com*

Lilleshall Human Performance Centre has been providing applied sports science and sports injury rehabilitation services for the past 16 years. We are home to the UKs only residential sports injury rehab centre:
tel: 01952 605828
email: info@lilleshall.com

As you would expect the LTA has a large number of contacts for tennis specific coaching and coach development. They can be found at:

The Lawn Tennis Association
Palliser Road
West Kensington
London, W14 9EG
tel: 020 7381 7000
website: www.lta.org.uk

For coaches who can provide more guidance on speed development you can contact the sprint coach at your local athletics club, or try the following organisations:

Amateur Athletic Association
Under 'development' on their website they have details of regional development coordinators and clubs.
tel: 0121 452 1500
website: www.englandathletics.org.uk

Regional contacts:

Northern Ireland Athletic Federation	tel: 028 906 02707
Scottish Athletics Federation	tel: 0131 317 7320
Athletic Association of Wales	tel: 01633 416 633
North of England Athletics Association	tel: 0113 246 1835
Midland Counties Athletics Association	tel: 0121 456 1896
South of England Athletics Association	tel: 0208 664 7244

UK Athletics
Under 'Clubs' you will find a great network of athletics clubs close to you
website: www.ukathletics.net

For coaches who can provide more guidance on weight training and weight lifting contact:

The British Weight Lifting Association
Lilleshall National Sports Centre
Newport,
Shropshire
TF10 9AT
tel: 01952 604201

NSCA — National Strength and Conditioning Association
An American site packed full of great info.
website: www.nsca-lift.org

For advice on finding a physiotherapist specialising in sports medicine:

The Association of Chartered Physiotherapists in Sports Medicine (ACPSM)
The ACPSM is the clinical interest group recognised by the Chartered Society of Physiotherapy, representing physiotherapists who have an interest and involvement in Sports Physiotherapy. On their website under 'regional reps' you will find contact details of someone near you throughout the UK.
website: www.acpsm.org

INDEX